A

NELSON

COMPANION

A
NELSON
COMPANION

A GUIDE TO
THE ROYAL NAVY OF
JACK AUBREY

C. MAYNARD

MICHAEL O'MARA BOOKS LIMITED

First published in Great Britain in 2004 by
Michael O'Mara Books Limited
9 Lion Yard
Tremadoc Road
London SW4 7NQ

Copyright © 2003, 2004 Michael O'Mara Books Limited
Formerly published, as *Ships' Miscellany: A Guide to the Royal Navy
of Jack Aubrey*, in 2003 by Michael O'Mara Books Limited

A CIP catalogue record for this book is available from the British Library

ISBN 1-84317-102-3

1 3 5 7 9 10 8 6 4 2

Designed and typeset by Design 23

Printed and bound in England by The Bath Press, Bath

CONTENTS

INTRODUCTION

The Royal Navy of the period from 1793 to 1815 – that is, from the declaration of war with Revolutionary France to the final defeat and capture of Napoleon after Waterloo – was undoubtedly the most successful organized military unit of its day. In the course of those years, the combined forces of Britain's Western enemies – principally the French, but also including at different times the Dutch, Spanish, Danes, Russians and Americans – destroyed or captured over 160 British warships; for its part, the Royal Navy defeated approximately 1,200 enemy vessels in the same period. Nor was it engaged solely in the European and North American conflicts, for it also transported and otherwise supported British forces in other areas of the world, helping to establish and secure the empire.

Britain's history as a maritime power has always exerted a considerable fascination, and at the core of that history lay the officers and men of the Royal Navy, as well as the great wooden warships on which they sailed. Books about the navy's history are plentiful, and have been since Nelson's day, while novels or series of novels based on life at sea in the last decade of the eighteenth century, and first decade of the nineteenth, have proved both remarkably successful and extremely enduring. Patrick O'Brian's highly regarded Aubrey-Maturin novels are the exemplars of fiction of this kind, but before them the 'Hornblower' novels of C. S. Forester, as well as other series by C. Northcote-Parkinson, Nathaniel Drinkwater, Alexander Kent and Dudley Pope (among others), have all proved highly popular with readers.

The Revolution in France that began in 1789 sent shockwaves through its European neighbours, who feared its anti-monarchic attitude would prove contagious and provoke serious civil unrest closer to home. The attack on a Royal Navy ship at Brest (see p.96) in 1793 by French shore batteries was the touchpaper that finally lit a declaration of war between the British and the French. Until the temporary peace of the Treaty of Amiens in 1802, the last decade of the eighteenth century was a continual round of shifting allegiances, political manoeuvrings and outright warfare, which modern historians have divided into seven 'Coalitions'. Jack Aubrey's Royal Navy faced opposition on almost every front; from the French, the Spanish, the Dutch, the Danish, and even from nations further afield such as America and Russia. In 1802 Napoleon re-established order in France and the Napoleonic Wars began, ostensibly to preserve the changes wrought by the Revolution, but increasingly manifested as Napoleon's personal ambition. The Royal Navy never ceded naval superiority even against the combined military might of several nations, and when Napoleon was captured in 1815 after his defeat at Waterloo, Britain filled the resultant power gap and ruled the waves for more than a hundred years.

This book is not a guide to the Aubrey-Maturin novels of Patrick O'Brian; nor is it a history, and far less a study, of the Royal Navy of Jack Aubrey's time. Instead, it is a miscellany, a collection of interesting, arcane, or extraordinary information about life at sea in the heyday of fighting sail. By 1815, those days were already numbered. In 1817, the Royal Navy took delivery of its first steam-powered vessel; in 1819 the American paddle-wheeler *Savannah* became the first steamship to cross the Atlantic; and in 1822 the first iron steamship made her maiden voyage. Although square-rigged ships would continue to be built as merchant vessels for many years to come, the writing, at least where warships were concerned, was on the wall.

In 1839 the great J. M. W. Turner first exhibited his much loved painting, known as *The Fighting Temeraire* but properly titled *The Fighting Temeraire, tugged to her Last Berth to be broken up*. Famously, it shows HMS *Temeraire* (98), one of the last surviving first rates that had fought at Trafalgar, being towed up the Thames to a shipbreaker's yard at Rotherhithe in September 1838, not quite thirty-three years after Nelson's outstanding victory. The towing vessel is a steam-powered paddle-wheel tug, belching out smoke with the great three-decker, still with her masts and yards but with no sail set, looming behind her. *Temeraire*, the second ship, behind *Victory*, in Nelson's column at Trafalgar, had gone to the flagship's aid during the battle, and had captured two French line-of-battle ships, including *Victory*'s opponent *Redoutable*. Of the painting, Ruskin wrote that it was 'the best memorial that Turner could give to the ship which was the *Victory*'s companion in her closing strife', while Thackeray thought Turner's view melancholic, writing, 'slow, sad and majestic, follows the brave old ship, with death, as it were, written upon her'. In the end, the painting symbolized the end of an era, for while, for a time, the navy's warships would continue to have sails as well as steam engines, the age of the square-rigged wooden warship was over, superseded by iron and steam.

The legacy of the age of fighting sail remains with us today, however, and not only in novels like O'Brian's, or films, or works of non-fiction. A great number of everyday English expressions still in common use derive directly from the sailing ships, merchant as well as naval, of the Georgian era, and the experience of the men who served them. It is hoped that this compact book has captured something of that era, and of the extraordinary world in which its seamen lived, fought and, often, died.

COMPILERS' NOTE

Anyone interested in the Royal Navy of Georgian times will quite quickly discover that even the most respected sources do not always tally with each other. (As an example, one leading naval historian states that there were seven crimes punishable by mandatory death sentence under the Articles of War, while another states that there were eight.) The figures and statistics given in this text, therefore, may not always be the same as those found in some other works, although they are likely to be close enough. Finally, it is not always possible to give absolutely definitive figures for such variables as gun ranges, speeds, ships' complements, and rates of fire, and those given here are in some cases 'best estimates' based on the available sources.

SHIPS

The warships of Jack Aubrey's era were built from wood and propelled by sails (the exception to the latter being oared war galleys, of which a few were still in service, though not in the Royal Navy, as late as the 1790s). The Royal Navy's warships were 'rated' according to their size and armament, and were divided into 'line-of-battle' ships (that is, ships large and powerful enough to join the battle line in a full-scale naval action; the post-Napoleonic-era word 'battleship' is a contraction of 'line-of-battle ship'), 'below-the-line' ships (which included frigates), and unrated vessels (which included sloops of war, gun boats and gun brigs, bomb vessels and fireships, cutters and schooners). The rated vessels were all three-masted, square-rigged ships, built mainly of oak, but they differed greatly in size, armament and configuration, as there was little standardization in the Georgian navy, while a programme of almost constant ship-building saw designs altered and refined over the years. In addition, many Royal Navy warships were in fact captured enemy vessels that had been pressed into British service. All rated ships were commanded by 'post-captains', since these vessels were known as 'post-ships'; a captain's seniority dated from when he 'made post', that is, took command of his vessel.

RATING OF SHIPS

Line of battle
First rate   3 gundecks, 100 guns or more
Second rate   3 gundecks, 90–98 guns
Third rate   2 gundecks, 64, 74 or 80 guns

Below the line
Fourth rate   1 or 2 gundecks, 50 guns
Fifth rate (frigates)   1 gundeck, 32–44 guns
Sixth rate (frigates)   1 gundeck, 20–28 guns

Unrated
Ship-sloops   1 gundeck, up to 22 guns
Brig-sloops   1 gundeck, up to 28 guns
Others   1 gundeck, up to 18 guns

FRIGATES

While it is tempting to concentrate on the great line-of-battle ships, the three- or two-decked first, second and third rates, the most exciting vessels were the fast and manoeuvrable frigates, referred to by Nelson as 'the eyes of a fleet'. In general these were used for reconnaissance and to engage smaller enemy vessels in individual actions; during a fleet engagement, however, they were usually deployed beyond the battle line to convey signals, although by the time of Trafalgar in 1805, the more modern larger frigates such as those of the *Leda* class, of thirty-eight 18-pounder guns, were increasingly used to rescue battle-damaged ships, to open attacks upon enemy movements away from the main action, to secure prizes, and to act opportunistically on their captains' initiative to attack or harass enemy vessels. One of the most famous frigates of the era was HMS *Shannon*, a fifth-rate, 38-gun 18-pounder frigate, which, on 1 June 1813, attacked and took the 50-gun American frigate *Chesapeake* in a brief but bloody action that lasted only some eleven minutes. (In O'Brian's *The Fortune of War* [1979], Aubrey is present at this action aboard the *Shannon*.) This victory did much to restore the navy's pride, for three of its fifth-rate frigates, as well as a number of smaller ships, had fallen to the Americans during the anomalously named 'War of 1812', and notably to the great American fifth-rate frigate USS *Constitution* (44). Built in 1797 and still in service with the US Navy, 'Old Ironsides', as the *Constitution* was nicknamed, is the oldest warship still afloat. (The 100-gun British first rate HMS *Victory*, Nelson's flagship at Trafalgar, launched in 1765, is the oldest warship still in commission; however, she has been in dry dock since the 1920s.)

SHIPS' COMPLEMENTS

First rates	841 officers and men
Second rates	743 officers and men
Third rates	494–724 officers and men
Fourth rates	345 officers and men
Fifth rates	217–297 officers and men
Sixth rates	138–198 officers and men
Ship-sloops	121–135 officers and men
Brig-sloops	80–121 officers and men
Others	variable, as sizes of craft differed greatly; an armed sloop would have a crew of 42

TYPES OF FRIGATE

Fifth rate

Number of guns		Complement
44 guns	20 18-pdr, 22 12-pdr, 2 6-pdr	250–280 officers and men
38 guns	28 18-pdr, 10 12-pdr and 9-pdr	250 officers and men
36 guns	26 12-pdr (later 18-pdr), 10 12-pdr and 9-pdr	240 officers and men
12-pounder 32 guns 26 12-pdr, 6 6-pdr		220 officers and men
18-pounder 32 guns 26 18-pdr, 6 6-pdr		220 officers and men

Sixth rate

Number of guns		Complement
28 guns	28 9-pdr	200 officers and men
22 guns	22 9-pdr, 8 24-pdr carronades, 2 6-pdr	160 officers and men

WARSHIP CONSTRUCTION

The ships in which Jack Aubrey sailed – and against which he fought – were built almost entirely from wood. Most of the hull and major structural members were built from oak, although elm was used for deck planking and for the keel and stern post. Once a timber frame for the hull had been constructed, it was planked both inside and out in carvel fashion – that is, with the planks laid edge to edge, rather than overlapping, as in clinker-built vessels – after which the planks were caulked by ramming oakum (a fibrous substance made by untwisting old ropes) into the gaps and then covering the result with hot pitch; deck planking was treated in the same way. With the hull planked, supporting timbers for the ship's interior were added, followed by the decks; the hull was completed by the addition of the various rooms, lockers, hatches, companionways and other parts. Fittings such as bolts, brackets and linking plates were mainly of iron, but nails were of copper, and after 1779 the hull below the waterline was also sheathed with copper plates, to protect against shipworm and other marine creatures. (Vessels built before 1779, such as HMS *Victory*, launched in 1765, had their sheathing fitted retroactively during a major refit.)

British warships were built in the royal dockyards found at many naval bases around the country, or – especially in the case of frigates – by private contractors, although the latter's work was supervised by the royal dockyards, to which nearly completed vessels were transported for fitting out and to have the copper sheathing added.

MASTS, YARDS, RIGGING AND SAILS

With the hull complete, the three masts that were common to all rated men-of-war were added. Since these ships carried an enormous area of sail, it was not possible to use masts constructed from a single pole, since no tree grew tall enough or strong enough. The mast was therefore built in three sections, with the thickest and strongest section running down through the decks to the keel (in some smaller ships such as frigates, the mizzen mast, the smallest of the three, ended at the level of the lower deck).

SPARS
The wooden poles fixed to the masts and bowsprit – which included yards, booms and gaffs, to which the sails were attached – were then added. These were, in order from bow to stern and from upper to lower:

Bowsprit:
sprit topsail yard; jib boom (the upper section of the two-piece bowsprit); spritsail yard; bowsprit

Foremast:
fore royal yard; fore topgallant yard; fore topgallant mast (the upper section of the three-part mast); fore topsail yard; fore topmast (the middle section of the mast); fore yard; foremast (the lowest section)

Mainmast:
main royal yard; main topgallant yard; main topgallant mast; main topsail yard; main topmast; main yard; mainmast

Mizzen mast:
mizzen royal yard; mizzen topgallant yard; mizzen topgallant mast; mizzen topsail yard; mizzen topmast; mizzen gaff; crossjack yard; mizzen boom; mizzen mast

With the masts and spars completed, the ship was rigged, which meant adding all the ropes, cables and chains used to support the masts and spars (standing rigging) and to raise, lower and adjust sails and yards (running rigging), as well as the tackle – pulley blocks, eyebolts and so on – needed to hold or adjust it. There were literally miles of rigging in a

rated warship, but it was essential to the ship, and included shrouds and stays (shrouds supported the masts and ran from the ship's sides, and in their two lower sections included ratlines, which functioned as rope ladders for men going aloft; stays also supported the masts, but ran fore-and-aft – a stay running forward towards the bow is a forestay, and one running towards the stern is a backstay).

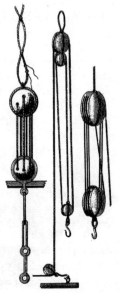

With the standing rigging completed, the sails and running rigging were added. The former were attached to the yards at the top, and could be furled or unfurled by men sent aloft for the purpose, or raised, lowered or otherwise adjusted by means of the running rigging. Sailing a large three-masted man-of-war was therefore a formidably complex business, and the training of officers and crew in handling sails and rigging was central to good shiphandling and seamanship.

SAILS OF A TYPICAL SQUARE-RIGGED SHIP

Sails were made from canvas, and were made up by the sailmaker, often aboard ship; spare canvas was carried on board while at sea, and a part of life on any warship was the care and repair of sails or, sometimes, making up new ones.

The principal sails were, from fore to aft and upper to lower:

flying jib	main topgallant staysail
jib	maintopsail
fore topmast staysail	mainsail or course
fore staysail	mizzen topgallant staysail
fore topgallant	mizzen topmast staysail
fore topsail	mizzen staysail
foresail or course	mizzen topgallant
main topgallant staysail	mizzen topsail
middle staysail	spanker
maintopmast staysail	mizzen sail
mainstaysail	

This was a standard set of sails, but others such as jibs and skyscrapers could be added as circumstances required.

FITTING OUT

With the standing rigging added, a ship would be fitted out by the addition of all the ancillary equipment, including the rudder and wheel, anchors and their cables (most rated ships carried four large anchors as well as a number of lighter ones), capstans (simple man-powered winches used to raise the anchors and for heavy work such as lifting, via pulleys, yards or guns), the ship's boats (ships of the line carried six: the captain's barge, a launch, a pinnace, two cutters and a jolly boat; these were used principally for ferrying men and stores, and for going ashore or to visit other ships, far more than they were intended as lifeboats), the galley stove and other such equipment, and pumps (for all wooden sailing vessels leaked, despite the caulking of the seams between the planking; a ship damaged during an engagement might leak very heavily, in which case the bosun would pipe 'All hands to the pumps', another nautical expression still in daily figurative use). The ship's armament (see later, pp.33–49) was also added, together with all its tackle and implements. At roughly the same time, the cabins and quarters, galley, magazine and store rooms were added to the interior, until, with the building complete, the ship was ready to be launched. She would then be 'put into commission' (that is, taken on for active service), at which point all her stores would be added. Commissioning did not necessarily follow directly upon completion of a ship, however; *Victory*, launched in 1765, was not commissioned until 1778.

CABINS AND QUARTERS

During Aubrey's time, the ship's cabins, i.e. rooms set aside for the officers' personal living space, were usually to be found at the stern. Aboard ships-of-the-line, the gunroom housed the lower-status officers, such as the gunner or chaplain, the space under the quarterdeck housed the wardroom officers, while the quarterdeck itself was occupied by the captain. Under the forecastle were cabins for the boatswain, cook and carpenter, though after 1801 the sick bay moved to this location.

The captain and wardroom officers both had unusual roommates – cannon. During battle the dividing walls between their cabins were dismantled so that the gun crews could work effectively.

The majority of the seamen slept below decks, amidships and forward. The conditions were often dire, with men cramped together (see p.92 for the space allocated to each hammock), poor ventilation and lighting; in such close proximity it was inevitable that disease, and rats, were prevalent. The marines' quarters were little better, but they were located between the officers and the crew and therefore slept apart from the majority of the seamen.

NAUTICAL ORIGINS OF
COMMON PHRASES AND SAYINGS – 1

Aback – to be taken aback
A dangerous situation when the wind veers or backs so that it is the wrong side of the sails, pressing them back against the mast and forcing the ship suddenly to slow, often with drastic consequences.

Back and fill
To work the sails so as alternately to fill and empty them of wind, a technique of tacking employed when the tide is with the ship but the wind against it, or when manoeuvring in a narrow space.

Barrel – to be over a barrel
A sailor about to be flogged was tied either to a grating, one of the masts, or over the barrel of a deck cannon.

Bear down
To sail downwind rapidly towards another ship or landmark.

Berth – to give (someone or something) a wide berth
The berth is a ship's anchoring or mooring place. So that ships did not hit each other when they swung with the wind or tide it was necessary to anchor or moor them far enough apart.

OFFICERS AND SEAMEN

The company of a Royal Navy vessel was a complex web of rank and discipline, more subtle than the initial assumptions one could infer might exist through class difference. As N.A.M. Rodger notes, across the ship's complement 'lay the invisible distinctions of social class, distributing gentlemen and tradesmen, noblemen and artisans with careless impartiality among the ranks and ratings'. Broadly speaking, however, the Royal Navy was divided into four 'classes', headed by commissioned officers, who formed the upper echelons of the naval hierarchy. The ranking went as follows, with the three colours representing the three different naval squadrons:

Admiral of the Fleet
Admiral of the Red (rank created after 1805)
Admiral of the White
Admiral of the Blue
Vice Admiral of the Red
Vice Admiral of the White
Vice Admiral of the Blue
Rear Admiral of the Red
Rear Admiral of the White
Rear Admiral of the Blue
Commodore (a temporary position for a
    captain put in charge of a squadron)
Captain
Master (and Commander)
    ('commander' was introduced in 1794,
    after which one could only become a
    captain after being a commander)
Lieutenant

Under the commissioned officers were the warrant sea officers, who possessed an official certificate of appointment (a 'warrant') from an authority such as the Navy Board, Ordnance Board, or Victualling Board, and who were in charge of specific duties on board, such as surgery or pursery. Some examples of warrant officers:

> Master
> Surgeon
> Purser
> Chaplain
> Boatswain
> Gunner
> Carpenter

Petty officers were also often warrant officers, and therefore had status above the ordinary ratings, but supported rather than headed the various specialists on board, and could be disrated or promoted at the captain's whim. As many petty officers were primarily artisans rather than seamen, they could not be pressed into service by the navy, and therefore awarding them a warrant and the resultant status may have been a ploy to lure them to serve. Petty officers serving in the Royal Navy included:

> Armourer and mates
> Gunner's mates
> Sailmaker and mates
> Yeoman of the powder room
> Cook
> Schoolmaster
> Purser's steward
> Captain's clerk
> Carpenter's mates
> Surgeon's mate
> Master-at-arms
> Quartermasters and mates
> Boatswain's mates

Finally, the 'private men' or seamen were either volunteers or the spoils of the 'press gangs', and were divided into three classes – able seamen, ordinary seamen, and landsmen. Able seamen were judged competent at seamanship and might, in time, invite promotion to the status of petty or warrant officers; ordinary seamen were inexperienced or perhaps often just incompetent, and landsmen had no sea experience at all. These men operated the rigging, hoisted and lowered the sails, rowed the ship's boats, rigged tackle, swabbed the decks, and did all the practical work and labour involved in running the ship under the orders of the commissioned, warrant, and petty officers.

Often making up 10 per cent of the ship's company, also to be found on board were servants, who were allocated to every officer on board. Boatswains, gunners and carpenters were allowed two, and the captain entitled to four for every hundred of the ship's complement. Often no more than boys, they were not as servants would be thought of now, but more like apprentices who were also on hand to provide menial service to their appointed officers when required.

Finally, a ship's complement included a detachment of marines. Formed in 1755, on the eve of the Seven Years War and under the control of the Admiralty rather than the War Office, they performed as infantry in sea-based operations. (See pp. 42-3).

SOME DISCIPLINES TAUGHT TO OFFICERS IN TRAINING AT THE ROYAL NAVAL COLLEGE, PORTSMOUTH, UK, IN THE EARLY NINETEENTH CENTURY

Seamanship	Navigation	Mathematics	Physics
Astronomy	Gunnery	Fortification	

DUTIES OF SHIP PERSONNEL

Admiral
The division of the Royal Navy into the squadrons, Red, White and Blue (in that order of seniority, with Red the greatest) was retained for the purpose of admiral's ranks, even though after 1794 the navy could be split into as many squadrons as was thought necessary. Admiral of the Fleet became an honorary position after 1805, when Admiral of the Red was introduced. Promotion was by seniority but did not necessarily happen in degrees, and did not necessarily mean holding command of a ship. An admiral's ship was called a flagship, and consequently a captain in charge of this ship was a flag-captain. *Blue at the Mizzen*, the last in the Aubrey-Maturin novels, sees Aubrey at long last becoming an admiral.

Commodore
This rank was simply a captain who held a temporary command over a squadron, and thus this gave him a similar authority to that of a rear admiral. Once their squadron duty was completed, they reverted to the rank of captain.

Captain
A captain was in charge of everyone, and everything, on board his vessel. Responsible for finding their own crews, captains could rate and disrate the ratings and the petty officers and were ultimately responsible for judging and sentencing crewmen for punishment. The 'happiness' of a crew depended a great deal on the temperament and nature of its captain – some led benignly, or through example, while others relied on discipline or beatings to see their orders carried out. A post-captain, the rank Aubrey is promoted to in the novel of the same name when given command of HMS *Lively*, was a captain in charge of a ship of the first to sixth rates.

Lieutenant
Usually the only commissioned rank on board other than the captain, the lieutenant was an experienced seaman with at least six years' experience at sea (three as a midshipman) behind him. The number of lieutenants varied depending on the rate of the ship – a first-rate had eight, a fifth-rate, three. They had all passed an oral exam (which was not always completely objective), but successful lieutenants had also achieved a

commission to a particular vessel. On board, lieutenants generally were in charge of groups of men; all kept watch, some commanded a section of guns, oversaw an administrative department, or served as signal lieutenants. Once an officer had reached the rank of lieutenant, promotion was primarily based on merit or political (or other) influence.

Midshipmen

Often young gentlemen, midshipmen occupied a curious position in relation to the other seamen. While nominally they were lieutenants-in-training, they had often previously been rated only as 'boy', a recent ranking that had replaced the older title of 'captain's servant'. They assisted the officer of the watch, kept logs of the ship's navigation, and might take command of the ship's boats in operations such as cutting out. While they couldn't be publicly flogged like seamen, their youth, combined with a certain amount of power, often resulted in high spirits or boisterous behaviour towards the other men, for which they could be reprimanded. A midshipman had to serve at least three years in that position if he wished to become a lieutenant.

Master

A senior warrant officer, the master was responsible for the navigation of the ship – setting courses, finding the ship's position, and highlighting and noting down hazards in the ship's path. Additionally, he was in charge of stowing the hold (a bad job of which would adversely affect sailing qualities), the security and issuing of spirits and beer, setting up the sails and rigging, supervising the midshipmen, and keeping the ship's official log book. The master was a considerable figure on board, and usually the highest-paid officer after the captain.

Surgeon

Surgeons received a warrant from the Navy Board, having usually learned their trade before going to sea, often by apprenticeship rather than by acquiring a medical degree. Once appointed to a ship, he served as surgeon's mate (renamed 'assistant surgeon' in 1805) for a time before being granted the rank of surgeon. On board he served as a physician as well as a surgeon proper, with responsibility for all the sick, injured and wounded, officers and seamen alike, which gave him considerable status. In action, they took post in the ship's cockpit, and dealt with wounded and injured men in the order in which they arrived, rather than according to the severity of their injuries; as a result, surgeons became adept at assessing wounds and performing even major surgery, in cramped and often chaotic conditions, extremely fast, and it was by no means uncommon for an amputation to be performed in a few minutes.

Purser

The purser occupied the unusual position of being at once an official, as well as a private contractor. He was responsible for stocking, supplying and managing the ship's stores, including food, drink, clothing, bedding, and fuel (for cooking and lighting), and because the navy held back part of the sailors' pay for the purser's expenses (and because he was in a position to embezzle money from the navy), he was often among the most unpopular members of the crew. Pursers were supported by the purser's yeomen, or purser's stewards, and like surgeons, obtained equivalency with commissioned officers in 1808.

Chaplain

In order to follow the requirement of the Article of War that stated church services were to be performed every Sunday, a chaplain was present on board. Despite their hard and often dangerous lives, sailors by and large were not a religious demographic; their Sundays were often spent surreptitiously drinking or gambling. The chaplains' 'idle' status on board sometimes made them unpopular, and the more superstitious seamen considered them unlucky.

STANDING OFFICERS

Boatswains, gunners and carpenters were so-called 'standing officers', meaning that they stayed with their ship even when it was out of commission. It also meant that they could not be disrated by a commanding officer, but only by the admiralty.

Boatswain (bosun)

In essence, the boatswain supervised all activity and labour above deck. He would oversee sail maintenance, the cordage and rigging, secure the boats, booms and anchor, and report any defects to the officer of the watch. He also had the unenviable duty of keeping discipline among the crew; the boatswain and his mates would use starters and rope's ends to maintain a lively and 'enthusiastic' attitude to work, and also administered the floggings upon the captain's orders.

Gunner

Befitting his position as a standing officer, a gunner had served at least four years, and been approved of by a 'mathematical master' and three naval gunners. The gunner did not choose when to fire during action; that was the duty of the commissioned officers. However, it was his task to keep running as smoothly as possible the process of cleaning, loading and firing the guns, and looking after the armament when not in battle to ensure it performed optimally during a fight. The gunner was also responsible for the small-arms, such as muskets, and edged weapons, such as the cutlasses. A gunner received his warrant from the Ordnance Board.

Carpenter

Carpenters had, like surgeons, frequently learnt their trade on shore as apprentices, usually in a naval dockyard. On board he was mainly concerned with the maintenance of the yards, masts and hull, and the condition of all the wooden fittings. He obtained his warrant from the Navy Board.

NAUTICAL ORIGINS OF
COMMON PHRASES AND SAYINGS – 2

Bitter – the bitter end
The bitts (or 'riding bitts') at the ship's bow were huge oak posts to which the end of the anchor cable was fastened (other bitts were situated near the masts, and were used for securing ends of rigging). When all the anchor cable has been paid out the bitter end is reached.

Board – above board
Anything on or above the open deck; that is, something in plain view is above board.

Board – gone by the board
Anything that had gone overboard or which was seen floating past the ship was considered to be lost at sea.

Booby hatch
A booby hatch is a sliding cover that must be pushed away to allow means of access. Its meaning (principally American) of mental institution probably derives from the booby, a fish-eating seabird of the tropics and sub-tropics; 'booby' derives from Spanish *bobo* meaning silly (presumably from the sometimes, to sailors, comical behaviour of the bird), and thus in the end came to mean a stupid or childish person.

Buoyed up
Using a buoy to raise the bight (the part of a rope, cable or chain between the ends) of an anchor chain to prevent it from abrasion on the seabed.

By and large
'By' in this context means into the wind, and 'large' means with the wind: as in, 'By and large the ship handled very well.' Hence 'to sail by the wind' means to sail into it as nearly as can be managed, while 'sailing large' means to sail with the wind blowing from astern.

NAVIGATION, NAVIGATIONAL AIDS AND WATCH-KEEPING

Navigation was vital to the fleet. It was an essential skill for every sea officer, from midshipman to admiral. It was precisely this skill which separated the sea officers from the petty officers and common seamen, for navigation required basic literacy and a high degree of numeracy.

> BRIAN LAVERY, *Nelson's Navy: The Ships, Men and Organisation 1793–1815* (1989)

The three sciences – or arts – upon which the Royal Navy of Jack Aubrey's time depended were seamanship (which included not only ship-handling, but tactics), gunnery and navigation. As Brian Lavery noted, navigation was vital, for the consequences of navigational errors were often dire, the loss of Admiral Sir Cloudesley Shovell's ships off the Scilly Isles in 1707 (see p.93-4) being just one example of what could happen through inaccurate or slipshod navigation.

DEAD RECKONING

In the days before accurate charts, wireless, satellite-navigation systems and all the other technological advances of the last 200 years, sailing ships navigated by 'deduced reckoning', generally referred to as 'dead reckoning'. This was a process of calculating – deducing – a ship's position from its headings (as recorded in the ship's log) and the distance travelled, which was calculated by measuring the ship's speed and multiplying the result by the time travelled at the recorded speeds. The ship's speed was measured with an instrument, also known as a log. In essence, this was a shaped piece of wood to which was fastened a long (about 900 feet) length of light cord, knotted at precisely regular intervals along its length; the cord was wrapped round a freely rotating reel. The log was streamed over the stern and the line, once free of the ship's wake, allowed to run out, the number of knots being timed by a small sand glass usually of 28 seconds. If during the timed period the log line ran out six knots, then the ship was travelling at 6 nautical miles per hour – 6 knots. These readings were generally taken every half hour, and the speeds recorded; as a result, the distance travelled in a given period of time could be calculated with moderate reliability. When the average speed over, say, twelve hours was combined with the record of the ship's headings at given times in that twelve-hour period, it was possible to calculate on a chart the ship's position by dead reckoning; in good conditions a skilled navigator could generally do so to within a few miles.

THE COMPASS

The most important navigational aid on board a warship was the compass. At that time, the compass card was inscribed with 32 equidistant 'points of sailing', rather than degrees: the four 'cardinal points' (N, S, E and W), the four 'cardinal half-points' (NE, NW, SW and SE), and then twenty-four others, each of which was named (for example, south-south-west, east-south-east, and so on), and it was the job of the helmsman at the wheel to keep the ship on the heading on which he had been ordered to steer. There were usually two compasses on a man-of-war, housed in a 'binnacle', a box set on the quarterdeck ahead of the wheel, so that the helmsman could see the compasses; at night, the binnacle was lit by a lantern. By Jack Aubrey's day, the variations in compasses because of the distance, itself variable, between magnetic north (to which a compass points) and true north were known, and officers on Royal Navy vessels were trained to take account of these discrepancies when navigating. By using the compass in conjunction with a chart, a ship could be steered with a high degree of accuracy, especially in coastal waters, which at that time were far better charted than the open sea. Compasses were also essential when navigating at night, in fog or heavy weather, or in narrow coastal areas where land features might obscure a sight of the ship's course ahead.

CHARTS

Since navigation was the responsibility of the master, he also had charge of the ship's charts. These showed land features, hazards, depths, tides and currents, and so on, but in the late eighteenth century the world's oceans were at best sketchily mapped, and only regular routes and coastal areas had been charted with any great accuracy. Until 1795 naval charts were mainly produced by commercial companies, but in that year the Admiralty established the Hydrographic Office, with responsibility for producing new charts and updating existing ones, and for their issue to warships.

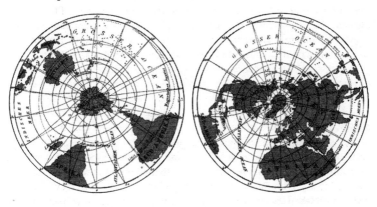

CELESTIAL NAVIGATION

While dead reckoning, as practised by a skilled master, could chart a ship's position with reasonable accuracy, the longer a voyage and the greater the distance from known land- or seamarks, the less accurate it became; in addition, the effects of, say, a severe storm could make it almost impossible to re-establish a ship's position with any certainty. As a result, officers were also trained in celestial navigation, the principles of which were based on the observations of moving bodies – the sun, moon and planets – relative to fixed ones – the stars. Since for centuries astronomers had been observing and 'mapping' the positions and movements of heavenly bodies, there was a substantial body of information available. Celestial navigation depended mainly upon measuring the angle of the sun relative to the horizon, and for this purpose a sighting would be taken each day at noon (when the sun is at its highest point) with a sextant, an extremely accurate instrument for measuring angles. With the observation of the height of the sun above the horizon at noon (duly corrected for certain known effects), a ship's latitude could be determined; by comparing the local noontime with noon at Greenwich (the 0-degree meridian), longitude could also be worked out. The latter measurement, however, depended upon the ship having an accurate timepiece unaffected by changes in temperature, humidity, or other local effects, or by the movement of the ship. Although such a timepiece, known as a chronometer (see below), had been perfected in the 1770s, they were extremely expensive, and in Aubrey's day few men-of-war had them – unless a ship's captain had paid for one himself. Sextant sightings were compared with information in the *Nautical Almanac*, published annually from 1765, which contained astronomical data that allowed officers to adjust their readings for time of year, area of the world, and so on, so increasing the accuracy of navigation. Celestial navigation was certainly more accurate than dead reckoning, but was at the mercy of the weather, since if the sun was obscured by cloud no sextant sighting could be taken, although it was also possible to take sightings at night from the moon and fixed stars. Using celestial sightings and calculations in combination with dead reckoning (as well as a good deal of figuring using trigonometry, logarithms and so on), however, it was possible for ships to be navigated with some accuracy when out of sight of land and even at considerable distances from their starting points.

TIMEKEEPING

The twenty-four-hour day aboard a man-of-war was divided into six 4-hour watches, although in practice it was seven watches, since the dog watch, from 16.00 hours to 20.00 hours, was subdivided into the first and last dog watches, each of two hours' duration, in order to ensure that the men did not stand their watches at the same time each day. The watches were:

Afternoon watch	12.00 hours to 16.00 hours
First dog watch	16.00 hours to 18.00 hours
Last dog watch	18.00 hours to 20.00 hours
First watch	20.00 hours to 00.00 hours
Middle watch	00.00 hours to 04.00 hours
Morning watch	04.00 hours to 08.00 hours
Forenoon watch	08.00 hours to 12.00 hours

The passage of each watch was measured by a 4-hour sand glass, and the watch was subdivided into eight 'glasses', which were measured by a $^1/_2$-hour sand glass. Each time the latter emptied it was turned by the midshipman of the watch and the marine sentry who guarded both sand glasses rang the bell, once for the first $^1/_2$ hour, twice for the hour, and so on up to 8 bells. Thus 3 bells of the forenoon watch is an hour and a half into the watch, that is, 09.30 hours, 4 bells of the morning watch is 06.00 hours, and 8 bells of the first watch is midnight. The sand glasses were kept outside the captain's cabin, under the permanent guard of a marine sentry.

1 bell	$^1/_2$ hour
2 bells	1 hour
3 bells	$1^1/_2$ hours
4 bells	2 hours
5 bells	$2^1/_2$ hours
6 bells	3 hours
7 bells	$3^1/_2$ hours
8 bells	4 hours

Accurate timekeeping was vital. John Harrison's marine chronometer, the final version of which was created in 1772, allowed accurate navigation by using the time to calculate a ship's longitude. Since the timepiece was prohibitively expensive to produce (and established seamen distrusted the technology), even as late as 1815 traditional methods of navigation and location-finding were still employed, with occasionally unpredictable results. Reference is made by Aubrey to the use of chronometers in *The Surgeon's Mate*.

NAUTICAL ORIGINS OF
COMMON PHRASES AND SAYINGS – 3

Cat – no room to swing a cat
The entire ship's company was required to witness floggings. As they gathered round, the bosun's mate might not have enough room to swing his cat-o'-nine-tails.

Cat – to let the cat out of the bag
The method of punishment for the more serious crimes in the Royal Navy – other than those punishable by death – was flogging. The whip used, called a cat-o'-nine-tails, was kept in a leather or baize bag. The cat consisted of nine knotted cords each about eighteen inches long fixed to a stout rope handle. Floggings were public and took place in front of the officers and crew. The transgressor, his back bared, would be tied to a mast, a grating or over the barrel of a gun, while a bosun's mate wielded the cat for the first half-dozen blows or so, after which he would be replaced by another man.

Chock-a-block
When two blocks (a block consists of one or more pulleys held in a wooden housing) of rigging tackle were so hard together that they couldn't be tightened further, they were said to be 'chock-a-block'.

Copper-bottomed
Utterly reliable; bound to succeed. The phrase derives from the copper sheathing used to protect wooden ships' hulls below the waterline.

Crow – as the crow flies
A crow released at sea will fly straight towards the nearest land. A ship's captain, if unsure of his closest landfall, would therefore order a caged crow to be set loose. Watching the direction of the bird's flight provided the vessel with the necessary navigational fix.

Cut and run
There are two possible origins of this saying. The first refers to the practice of cutting the lashings on all the sails and then running away before the wind, regardless of the direction in which that took the ship, a means of rapid retreat. The second meaning is to cut the anchor cable and sail away with despatch, also in order to make a quick escape.

GUNNERY – SHIPS AS GUN PLATFORMS

Given the elegance, even beauty, of square-rigged men-of-war in full sail, it is easy to forget that these were fighting machines and, for their date, extremely efficient ones. In essence, they were mobile gun platforms, for in the naval engagements of Aubrey's day, armament and gunnery were as important as seamanship. The weight of *Victory*'s broadside at Trafalgar – by which time she mustered 104 guns – was 1,148 pounds, or just over half a ton of iron shot discharged by all the guns on one side at a single firing. During that battle, *Victory* put the *Bucentaure* (80) out of action by treble-shotting her guns and firing on the French flagship as she passed; about an hour later, having suffered similar broadsides from other British ships as they too breached the enemy line, *Bucentaure*, by then a dismasted hulk, struck her colours, her admiral, Villeneuve, having tried unsuccessfully to transfer to another French ship.

In addition, there was no land machine capable of the speed of a warship – a fifth-rate frigate, for instance, could manage 13 knots (15 mph) with all sail. On land, only cavalry and horse artillery could achieve speeds of that order, and then only for very brief periods; at these speeds a man-of-war, given the right sailing conditions, could cover huge distances in what was, for those days, a very short time.

The principal armament of a man-of-war consisted of batteries of cannon arranged on one or more decks. Almost all the guns were sited to fire at right angles to the ship's axis through gun ports in its side. Being smooth-bore muzzle-loading weapons with relatively short barrels, the cannon had neither great range nor great accuracy; at the sort of ranges at which most naval engagements were fought, however, this was no disadvantage, for the guns fired enormous iron balls (commonly, in Aubrey's day, 12-, 18-, 24- or 32-pound round shot) or other projectiles at almost point-blank range, with devastating effect. On the whole the sciences of gunnery and ballistics were little studied or understood in the Royal Navy of Georgian times (something that was not true of the army's artillerymen), most commanders taking to heart Nelson's principle that 'no captain can do very wrong if he places his ship alongside that of an enemy.' At such close quarters, rate of fire was far more important than accuracy, and in this British gun teams excelled – a good gun crew could reload, aim and fire a 32-pounder twice in two minutes. The effects of large-calibre guns firing into a wooden ship at ranges sometimes of only a few feet can scarcely be imagined, and it is a tribute to the courage and endurance – and the discipline and morale – of officers and men alike that they stood up under such punishment again and again.

LONG GUNS

Cast-iron cannon known as 'long guns' formed the main armament of a rated man-of-war. Depending on the weight of the gun's projectile, these ranged in length of barrel from $c.$ $8^1/_2$ feet for a 12-pounder to $c.$ $9^1/_2$ feet for a 32-pounder (by 1805, the navy's heaviest long gun, the 42-pounder, was obsolete, though some were still found in fourth-rate ships), and weighed up to $2^3/_4$ tons. If a gun broke loose from the arrangement of ropes and pulleys that allowed the weapon to recoil and to be pulled back for reloading, it became a dangerous 'loose cannon' on the deck of a rolling and pitching ship, and had to be secured and restored to its position as quickly as possible, at considerable risk to the sailors.

Because of the danger of fire and explosion, powder charges were not kept with the guns, but were fetched individually by 'powder monkeys' from the ship's magazine in cylindrical wooden boxes each of which held a single powder cartridge or 'charge'; these cases varied in size depending on the calibre of the gun and the weight of the charge. Powder monkeys were boy sailors, often very young indeed to have so dangerous a job in battle.

GUN CREW

The crew of each long gun generally consisted of six men (seven for a 32-pounder), who were, in order of seniority:

> The captain of the gun
> The second captain
> The loader
> The sponger (or rammer)
> The assistant loader
> The assistant sponger

Up to nine more men, depending on the size of the gun, were required to man the breeching ropes, which checked the recoil, and the tackles for running out and training. They also acted as firemen, for water barrels were kept close by, fire being an ever-present danger.

NAVAL CANNON

A naval cannon of the type with which Jack Aubrey would have been familiar was a simple but extremely heavy artillery piece, with only limited provision for elevation and traverse. This latter was partly due to the fact that guns were trained through square gun ports in the ship's side, which necessarily limited the amount by which the barrel could be raised or lowered, or the gun swung from side to side. In practice, however, this was not much of a disadvantage, except when chasing a faster vessel, for the ranges at which naval actions were fought in Aubrey's day were measured often in yards, at which the guns would be firing 'point blank'. (The term has come to mean 'at extremely close range'; in actual fact, its technical meaning is a range at which there is no fall of shot from the point of aim; i.e. the weapon did not have to be elevated to increase its projectile's range. The point-blank range of a 32-pounder gun firing a standard charge of powder was about 400 yards).

Naval cannon were mounted, by means of 'trunnions' cast into the sides of the barrel, on wooden 'carriages', which allowed the barrel to be elevated or depressed by a certain amount. The gun carriage was itself mounted on four wooden wheels, or 'trucks', which permitted the piece to be wheeled backwards and forwards for reloading and firing, and also

allowed it a certain amount of rearward movement under recoil after firing; typically, the recoil distance of a 32-pounder gun after firing was 11 feet. The recoil of the gun was in fact used to the gunners' advantage, for it brought the piece back to a position from which it could be reloaded; when the gun was run out through the gun port, the loader could not reach the muzzle to conduct the operations for reloading. The recoil distance was limited by the 'breech rope' or 'breeching rope', a thick rope (some $2^1/_4$ inches in diameter for a 32-pounder gun) which looped through a ring at the breech end of the gun, and each end of which was fastened to eyebolts on the ship's side. The gun's movement back to the firing position – that is, the gun 'run out' with the muzzle protruding through the gun port – was effected by means of the 'gun tackles', a system of ropes and pulleys anchored at one end, in the case of the 'side tackles', to each side of the carriage, the other end being fixed to eyebolts on the ship's side. A third tackle, called the 'train tackle', ran from the rear or 'train' of the carriage to an eyebolt in the deck behind the gun; this was used to prevent the gun from rolling back out through the gun port during reloading. On active service at sea, a ship's guns were kept loaded, the muzzle blocked against the ingress of water by a wooden plug known as a 'tampion' (or 'tompion'). At the breech end, the 'vent' (or 'touch hole') or, where fitted, the firing mechanism (see above), would be covered by a lead sheet tied down with tapes, as a result of which it was known as an 'apron'. When not in service, a cannon's breech, gun and train tackles were 'frapped' (lashed together), which prevented the gun from moving as the ship pitched and rolled, and a rope passed around the muzzle and lashed to two eyebolts above the gun port; the hinged gun port lid could then be closed to prevent seawater from entering through the port.

THE PARTS OF A NAVAL LONG GUN

(NB: the barrel tapered from breech to muzzle, being considerably narrower at the latter end)

muzzle
approximately the last one-sixth of the barrel; also, the end of the gun from which the projectile is discharged.

chase
the foremost half (roughly) of the barrel, from just ahead of the trunnions to the muzzle.

second reinforce
a thicker section of the barrel, roughly one-fifth of its overall length, bounded at each end by the second and first reinforce rings, and from which, at its foremost end, the trunnions protrude.

first reinforce
the section, thicker still than the second reinforce, from the first reinforce ring back to the base ring, just behind the vent, roughly one-quarter of the barrel's overall length.

cascable
the final one-tenth of the barrel, from the base ring (the widest part) back to the tip of the button.

breech
the rearmost end of a gun, built thicker than the muzzle to withstand the detonation of the charge, and containing the vent and, where fitted, the firing mechanism.

face
the flat end of the muzzle of a gun.

bore the internal width of the barrel.

trunnions
short axles protruding at right angles to the axis of the gun, cast integral

with the barrel and positioned just behind its mid-point. The barrel was secured to the carriage by clamps that bolted down over the trunnions, which in turn fitted into semicircular recesses in each side of the carriage; being circular in cross section, trunnions allowed the gun a measure of elevation and depression, since they could rotate within the half-round clamps and the recesses in the carriage.

vent
the touch hole at the breech end of the gun, drilled from the top of the breech down into the chamber that received the charge. Priming powder was poured down the vent; when lit, this ignited the main charge, so firing the gun.

button
an almost spherical casting or ball at the breech extremity of a cannon, tapering first to a wrist before widening to the base ring, the thickest part of a gun. A ring was cast into the wrist of the button at the upper side to take the breeching rope. The button could be used for lifting or moving a gun, since the wrist allowed a turn of rope to be wrapped round it.

gunlock
by Jack Aubrey's day, the old system of firing cannon by applying a burning slow match to priming powder at and around the vent was being replaced by spring-loaded gunlocks. These were in essence flintlock mechanisms similar to those that had been used on muskets and pistols for many years, and consisted of a hammer which held a flint at its upper end. The hammer was cocked against its spring and priming powder was added to the pan by the vent, into which a quill tube had been inserted; when the gun captain pulled the lanyard (cord) that served as a trigger, the hammer fell, causing the flint to strike sparks from the steel, which in turn ignited the powder in the quill tube, and thus the powder in the main charge. Gunlocks were safer and more reliable than the old slow-match method of firing, and meant that there was no longer a need to keep burning material – the match in its linstock (see p.49) – around the gun when it was in action.

CARRONADES

Invented in the late 1770s and developed by the Carron Iron Works in
Stirlingshire (after which it was named), the carronade first went into
service with the Royal Navy in 1779, although it would not go into
general service on British ships for another fifteen years or so. It was a
short cannon of relatively large calibre, and with a chamber narrower
than the actual calibre. The bore was more closely machined than in long
guns (in other words, there was much less of a gap, or 'windage', between
barrel and shot), which meant that the gun could use a smaller charge of
powder since much less of the force of the detonating charge was wasted.
Carronades were also lighter than cannon of the same calibre (a 68-
pounder carronade weighed about 1.65 tons, against the 2.75 tons of a
32-pounder long gun; a 32-pounder carronade weighed 0.85 ton), and
although their short barrels made them relatively inaccurate over longer
distances, in practice this was rarely a disadvantage, since naval
engagements were generally fought at short range. In addition, the
shortness of their barrels made them easier, and thus faster, to reload
than long guns. Carronades were built in a number of calibres, the
commonest being 24- and 32-pounders, and by the beginning of the
nineteenth century most ships, of whatever rating, carried them – at
Trafalgar, *Victory* carried two 68-pounder carronades in addition to her

main armament – while some brig sloops were designed to be armed with nothing else. Jack Aubrey's temporary command as a post-captain, the frigate HMS *Surprise*, carried twelve 32-pounder carronades on her quarterdeck and forecastle and twenty-two 12-pounder long guns on her upper deck.

Being lighter and shorter-barrelled than cannon, carronades were mounted on a special carriage that incorporated a slide to allow for recoil and reloading. This carriage had a pivot rather than wheels or 'trucks' at the front, and two small wheels set at right angles to the axis of the gun at the rear, which made traversing the weapon much easier than was the case with long guns, which had to be hand-spiked round. In place of the button, a horizontal threaded ring at the breech end of the barrel was equipped with a large elevating screw, thus dispensing with the long gun's quoin (see p.49). Gun tackles were similar to those on long guns, consisting of a breeching rope and two side tackles; since the pivot at the front of the carriage was fixed to the ship, there was no train tackle.

At short ranges carronades were devastating whether firing round shot or canister, and came to be known as 'smasher guns'. The French – even the Emperor himself – recognized the advantage these powerful yet light weapons gave the Royal Navy, but were fatally slow in developing their own versions.

CHASE GUNS or CHASERS

Relatively small-calibre long guns mounted on the bow to fire ahead from the forecastle ('bow-chasers'), or on the stern to fire from the quarterdeck or poop. Chasers, often 9-pounder or 6-pounder guns, were, although physically smaller, longer-barrelled in relative terms than conventional long guns, and were often built of brass, which could be machined to finer tolerances between bore and shot, so permitting greater accuracy. Bow-chasers were used to fire at long range at an enemy being pursued, in the hopes of hitting masts or rigging and so slowing or even disabling the escaping vessel. Stern-chasers were fired at a pursuing enemy ship, again in the hopes of damaging or crippling it, so ending the chase. The term 'chase guns' or 'chasers' was also used of long guns taken from the main armament and temporarily mounted at the bow of a ship.

SWIVEL GUNS

A small cannon mounted on a swivel, which allowed it to be fired at almost any angle. Loaded with loose lead shot, they were mainly used against human targets in close-range fighting. Often mounted on the ship's rail, they were sometimes taken aloft during an engagement and, with the gun mount lashed to a spar or even the rigging, used to fire down on to the enemy's deck. They could also be used to arm the ship's boats.

SMALL ARMS

Almost all Royal Navy warships in Jack Aubrey's day carried muskets, not only for use during engagements at sea, but also for protection – or even for shooting birds and animals for food – during forays ashore; by 1797, a line-of-battle ship carried around 130 flintlock muskets, besides the muskets carried by its contingent of marines. In action, muskets would be issued to some of the seamen, and they would be detailed either to go aloft and fire down on an enemy ship, or to shoot at the sharpshooters in the enemy's tops and rigging, or to fire volleys into an enemy ship's decks.

Similarly, such a ship would have had some seventy pistols aboard, as well as a large number of swords, pikes and poleaxes (a short-handled axe; one side of the blade is an axe head, the other a metal spike – these were sometimes called 'tomahawks'). These would have been issued to selected seamen and warrant officers (officers and some warrant officers had their own swords and, often, pistols; midshipmen were armed with dirks, a short sword somewhere between a dagger and a sword) before an engagement, and were used principally either in defending a ship against boarding, or in boarding an enemy, although the axes were in fact more useful in cutting rigging away than as weapons. The marines also had bayonets for their muskets.

MARINES

As has been said, ship's complement included a detachment of marines. Soldiers have served at sea since ancient times, but by the eighteenth century British warships on active service took with them a detachment of soldiers drawn from one of the regiments of infantry of the line, to serve as marines. By the middle of that century it became clear that a specialist corps of marines was required, essentially soldiers trained not only as infantry, but in fighting at sea and in amphibious operations on land, as when ships were sent to subdue, capture or reduce a shore-based enemy. In 1755, therefore, on the eve of the Seven Years War, what became the Corps of Royal Marines was formed under the direction and control of the Admiralty rather than the War Office, to perform as infantry in sea-based or sea-launched operations. The title Royal Marines was granted by royal warrant in 1802.

Being in essence specialized soldiers serving on board men-of-war, or at military dockyards and other naval shore establishments, the marines had two primary functions: ensuring order and discipline on board ship, and curbing any attempts at mutiny; and, secondly, engaging the enemy in boarding or sharpshooting actions, as well as helping to man the guns; other duties included acting as sentries and joining landing parties. They served as sentries outside the captain's cabin, the liquor room and the magazine, and kept order when punishments were carried out. While marines often made up over 20 per cent of a ship's complement they were not obliged to help out above board, although they often took part in the unskilled work. As marines were strictly landsmen, they could not be impressed, and many non-British nationals were recruited to make up for the shortage of men that plagued the British forces during the period in which the Jack Aubrey novels are set.

That same shortage of men meant that the corps of marines remained a relatively small formation for a considerable time, with the result that detachments of marines drawn from infantry regiments continued to serve at sea for many years after 1755. At the battle known as the Glorious First of June in 1794 (see p.96), for instance, men of the 29th Foot (later the Worcestershire Regiment, later still the Worcester and Sherwood Foresters Regiment) so distinguished themselves that they were awarded the honour of a naval crown, which was incorporated into the regimental badge.

RELOADING AND FIRING A NAVAL CANNON

Since guns were usually kept loaded at sea, they either had to be fired before they could be reloaded, or the shot and charge had to be 'drawn' from the barrel, an often tedious procedure. Once fired, and with the gun run back under recoil from the port to the reloading position and secured there by the tackles, the sequence was as follows:
  the gun captain inserts his priming wire in the vent
  the rammer 'worms and sponges' the gun to remove or

damp out any still-smouldering remains of the previous charge

the loader inserts a cartridge ('charge') followed by a wad into the muzzle

the rammer rams wad and cartridge home

the loader inserts a shot (or canister, bar shot etc. – see below) followed by another wad

the rammer rams the top wad home over shot and charge

the gun captain pricks the charge through the vent with his priming wire to promote ignition of the main charge by the priming charge

the gun captain pours priming powder into the trough at the vent or, since guns in Aubrey's day were increasingly fitted with flintlock firing mechanisms (see p.38), inserts a goose quill filled with fine powder into the vent

the gun crew and assistants run out the gun to the firing position by means of the gun tackles

if necessary, the gun crew use 'hand spikes' (see below) to alter the gun's position to left or right, and adjust the elevation by moving the 'quoin' (see p.49)

the order 'Fire!' is given: the gun captain either touches a slow match held in a 'linstock' (see p.49) to the priming powder at the vent, or pulls a lanyard to release the flintlock mechanism, which strikes a spark that ignites the powder in the quill tube

the gun runs back under recoil, is secured by the gun crew, and the sequence is repeated.

ORDERS FOR FIRING, RELOADING AND SECURING A NAVAL CANNON

In Jack Aubrey's day, according to the Historical Maritime Society (www.hms.org.uk), the sequence of fifteen orders issued by the gun captain for firing a single shot, clearing, reloading and securing the gun (assuming that it was already loaded and secured before firing) was as follows:

> Silence!
> Cast loose your gun!
> Level your gun!
> Take out your tampion!
> Prime!
> Run out your gun!
> Point your gun!
> Fire!
> Worm and sponge!
> Load with cartridge!
> Load with shot and wad to your shot!
> Ram home shot and wad!
> Put in your tampion!
> House your gun!
> Secure your gun!

PRINCIPAL TYPES OF SHOT

Since exploding shells were not used in naval warfare at this date except by bomb vessels, which fired fused shells from the mortars they carried, the projectiles fired by long guns and carronades were solid shot, almost invariably of iron, given that lead was far more expensive.

round shot
the standard cannon ball, cast in iron. The most common form of shot carried by Royal Navy men-of-war, solid round shot was used against enemy ships and to bombard shore batteries and other land-based targets.

chain shot
two round shot or half shot linked by a short length of chain and used to wreck masts, yards, rigging and sails. Also called double-headed shot.

bar shot
two half shot joined by a rigid bar, also used against rigging etc.

canister
also called canister shot or case shot: a cylindrical tin or iron container, made just smaller than the bore of the gun, containing a number of smaller iron balls (each of 3 pounds, in the case of a 32–pounder) arranged around a central wooden core; used for general destruction and against human targets.

grape
also called grape shot: a number of small iron or lead balls, from 1–2 inches in diameter depending on the size of the gun, arranged around an iron spindle with a circular base at its lower (breech) end and sewn into a canvas container of approximately the gun's bore; fired mainly against human targets, ship's boats etc. Both canister and grape worked like a charge of pellets from a shotgun, and could be extremely effective against groups of enemy attempting to board and similar 'soft' targets.

hot shot
also called red-hot shot: in essence, a round shot that had been raised to red heat in a special furnace, then loaded into a cannon and fired at an enemy ship or other combustible target. Mainly used by shore batteries, it being easier to site the furnace on land, as well as to load the glowing projectile into the gun, nevertheless some ships did carry a furnace and use hot shot in action. Loading was tricky: two men carried the red-hot shot in special tongs to the gun, which had been loaded with a charge over which a damp wad, sometimes of wet clay, had been rammed home – this was to prevent the shot 'cooking off' the powder charge prematurely. A second wad would be swiftly rammed home over the shot and the gun trained and fired. Carrying out these operations on the often slippery deck of a pitching and rolling ship in the middle of an engagement required skill as well as courage of a very high order; nevertheless, a red-hot shot lodged in an enemy ship's planking would almost certainly start a fire, and if such a round penetrated one of the powder magazines the result would be catastrophic.

Shot was stored in lockers, of which there were generally three in rated ships, positioned fore, amidships and aft. Although not in any way volatile, it had to be protected from water, as shot caked in rust would often not fit the gun's bore.

POWDER

This was 'black powder', a composite of sulphur, saltpetre (potassium nitrate) and fine charcoal rendered granular by a process called 'corning'. It came in different degrees of fineness (big guns using the coarsest and small weapons like pistols the finest, which was also used for priming), and on board ship was made up by crewmen into charges for the guns, which were cartridges of cloth or paper of varying sizes, depending upon the power of the charge; a full charge for a 32-pounder contained 11 pounds of powder, a reduced charge 6 pounds, and a saluting charge 6 pounds.

Black powder – self-evidently – although a relatively stable compound, is highly combustible, and is easily detonated by a mere spark. On board a warship, therefore, it was stored in a magazine set deep in the vessel and well away from any source of fire or sparks; it also had to be protected from water, since damp powder would not ignite. Magazines were specially constructed, and were adjacent to the 'filling room', where cartridges were made up. No iron implements were permitted anywhere near the powder, which was stored loose in wooden barrels bound with copper or wooden hoops, rather than the more usual iron ones. Also adjacent was a 'light room', an entirely separate compartment in which were set lanterns to light the magazine and filling room through glass-paned windows, since in those days lanterns and candles were the only practical source of artificial light. In almost every case, fire in a ship's magazine would result in the destruction of the vessel.

When fired, black powder gave off a dense cloud of white smoke which, in relatively windless conditions, could hang over an engagement and add further to the confusion of battle, the so-called 'fog of war' (an expression that originated during the Napoleonic Wars). In action, the gunners' faces would become black with smoke and unburned powder residue, while the fumes made them extremely thirsty and often induced headaches, which were in turn exacerbated by the report of the gun firing and the general din of battle; they also often suffered 'powder burns', caused when burning powder grains from the discharge landed on the skin of their faces, hands and arms. Black powder continued to be used until well into the last quarter of the nineteenth century, when it was superseded by the invention and refinement of 'smokeless powder', which not only made almost no smoke on firing, but which was also a considerably more powerful propellant than black powder.

GUN IMPLEMENTS

The gunner's stores contained spare parts and tools for servicing the guns, even including a small forge that could be set up ashore. The gun implements were kept on the gun deck with each weapon, and were used during training and in action.

apron
a thin sheet of lead equipped with tapes, with which it was tied over the vent of a gun when the weapon was not in service, to keep water and foreign matter out. On guns equipped with gunlocks, an apron specially adapted to fit round the mechanism and cover the vent was used.

hand spike
a wooden stave, circular in section at the 'hand' end and square at the other, used to lever the gun carriage round in order to alter the weapon's point of aim relative to the ship's centre line; hand spikes also doubled as the staves inserted into a windlass and by which it was turned.

linstock
a wooden staff with a forked end, used for holding the slow match which, on guns not equipped with firing mechanisms, was applied to the priming at the vent to fire the weapon.

quoin
a wooden wedge on the gun carriage beneath the breech end of the gun. The barrel was weighted so that it tended to elevate the muzzle; the quoin was pushed forward to depress the barrel, and moved rearwards to elevate it.

rammer
a long-handled wooden implement with a wooden head slightly smaller than the gun's bore; used to ram home charge, wad and shot.

rope (or flexible) rammer
an immensely thick length of rope with a wooden rammer head at one end and a sponge head at the other; in the restricted space on a gun deck, this was extremely useful, since the flexible rope needed much less space ahead of the muzzle than the wooden-handled rammers and sponges.

sponge
a long-handled wooden implement with a wooden head covered in sheepskin; after firing, this was dipped in water and run through the barrel to damp out any still-smouldering remains of the previous charge and wadding, which might 'cook off' the new charge.

tampion (or **tompion**)
a wooden disk, slightly tapered, that was pressed into the muzzle of a gun when it was not in service to keep out water; it was usually heavily greased with tallow to effect an air- and watertight seal.

wadhook
a wooden-handled implement with an iron 'worm' (screw), in this case a kind of double corkscrew, at one end, used for extracting wads and charges from an unfired gun by screwing the hook into the wad or charge and pulling it back up the barrel.

worm
similar to the wadhook, and used during reloading to remove any remains of the cartridge bag from the previous firing that might still be in the gun and which, apart from providing a restriction to the new charge, might still be smouldering.

NAUTICAL ORIGINS OF
COMMON PHRASES AND SAYINGS – 4

Devil – between the devil and the deep blue sea
The devil seam was the seam in the deck planking closest to the side of the ship. If a sailor slipped on the deck, he could find himself between the devil and the deep blue sea. *See also* Devil – the devil to pay

Devil – the devil to pay
To 'pay' the deck seams meant to seal them with tar (caulking). The devil seam at the side of the ship was the most difficult to pay because it was curved and intersected with the straight deck planking. The ship's waterline seam was also known as the devil, and was equally hard to caulk. *See also* Devil – between the devil and the deep blue sea

Dressing down
'Dressing down' was the process of treating old or worn sails with oil or wax to refurbish them and make them water-resistant. An officer or seaman who was severely reprimanded was said to have received a dressing down.

First rate etc.
British naval ships were rated as to the number of heavy cannon (long guns) they carried (carronades and small cannon were not included in the listing of the number of guns carried). First rates mounted 100 or more guns; second rates 90 to 98 guns; third rates 64 to 89 guns; fourth rates, 50 to 60 guns; and frigates carrying between 20 and 48 guns were either fifth- or sixth-rated. (See RATING OF SHIPS, p.11). Originally, therefore, to call something 'fifth-rate', for example, did not necessarily mean that it was inferior, merely smaller or less powerful.

Fly-by-night
A large sail used only for sailing downwind which required little attention.

Footloose
The foot is the bottom portion of a sail. If it is not secured it flaps in the wind.

FOOD AND DRINK

Englishmen, and more especially seamen, love their bellies above anything else, and therefore it must always be remembered in the management of the victualling of the Navy that to make any abatement in the quantity or agreeableness of the victuals is to discourage and provoke them in the tenderest point, and will sooner render them disgusted with the King's service than any other hardship that can be put upon them.

SAMUEL PEPYS, SECRETARY TO THE ADMIRALTY, 1672–9 and 1684–8

To ensure the smooth running of life and work on board ship, and to keep morale high, it was essential that the men were given enough food and drink of good enough quality each and every day to keep them both satisfied and well-nourished. However, it was a challenging feat to make sure that each ship had adequate rations of every foodstuff before setting sail on a long voyage, and it was the Victualling Board, which had its own bakeries, breweries and slaughterhouses, which was responsible for such an important task.

STANDARD WEEKLY RATION OF FOODSTUFFS PER MAN ISSUED BY THE VICTUALLING BOARD

	Bread	Beef	Pork	Pease	Oatmeal	Butter	Cheese	Beer
Sunday	1 lb	—	1 lb	$^1/_2$ pt	—	—	—	1 gal
Monday	1 lb	—	—	—	1 pt	2 oz	4 oz	1 gal
Tuesday	1 lb	2 lbs	—	—	—	—	—	1 gal
Wednesday	1 lb	—	—	$^1/_2$ pt	1 pt	2 oz	4 oz	1 gal
Thursday	1 lb	—	1 lb	$^1/_2$ pt	—	—	—	1 gal
Friday	1 lb	—	—	$^1/_2$ pt	1 pt	2 oz	4 oz	1 gal
Saturday	1 lb	2 lbs	—	—	—	—	—	1 gal

The type of bread that was made specially for consumption at sea differed considerably from that of a conventional loaf, being hard and crumbly, not unlike a biscuit. Known as 'ship's biscuit' it was baked and packed up at the Victualling Office on Tower Hill, by the Thames in London. To preserve the rations of beef and pork, the meats were salted and pickled in casks. Other foodstuffs, many of which were supplied dried, were also packed in casks, including butter, cheese, flour, stockfish (dried cod), vinegar, suet, raisins, oatmeal, pease and oil.

The Admiralty was tremendously thorough in its efforts to make sure that its seamen were 'supplied with the best of everything in its kind', and that casks of certain rations were not kept in supply for too long a time; for example, a cask of pork or beef could only be stored for a maximum of two years.

Though it appears that a seaman's average diet was basic, limited and fairly sparse, the meals contained more than enough calories for the men to complete a hard day's physical work on a navy vessel. In fact compared to the diet of the poor on land, sailors fared very well, with a hot meal every day and at least four portions of meat per week.

Although the officers were entitled to eat the same basic food as the men, they only usually did so when their money or their own supplies ran out. Standard practice among the officers was to take it in turns to buy in food and wine for their mess, which was prepared by their own cook. They could also pay for fresh food, such as chickens, pigs and sometimes even cows that were kept on board.

VARIETIES OF CHEESE PURCHASED BY THE NAVY

Suffolk cheese
A 'flet' cheese which was made from skimmed cow's milk, it was also known as 'Suffolk Bang', and mentioned by Samuel Pepys who complained that his servants wouldn't eat it. A well-known eighteenth-century saying pertained to the hard, thin, and virtually inedible consistency of the cheese: 'Hunger could break through anything except Suffolk cheese,' as well as a rhyme that went: 'Mocks the weak effort of the bending blade, Or in the hog-trough rests in perfect spite, Too big to swallow, and too hard to bite.'

Cheshire cheese
In response to the number of complaints received about the generally poor quality of Suffolk cheese, in 1758 the navy decided to change varieties to Cheshire and Gloucester (see below), despite the fact that they did not last as long and were more expensive. The full-cream variety of Cheshire cheese was quite dry, crumbly, and slightly salty, but more fatty and nourishing.

Gloucester cheese
Most of the Gloucester cheeses issued to the navy were probably single Gloucester, a 'flet' cheese similar to Suffolk, but generally considered softer and more palatable.

In addition to standard rations, there also existed an accepted system of substitute foodstuffs for usual items that became unavailable when supplies had run low:

SUBSTITUTE FOODSTUFFS AND THEIR TYPICAL EQUIVALENT TO STANDARD RATIONS

1 pt wine *or* $^1/_2$ pt arrack, rum or brandy = 1 gal beer
3 lbs flour + 8 oz suet = 1 piece of beef (equivalent to 4 lbs)
3 lbs flour + 8 oz raisins + 4 oz suet = 1 piece of beef
2 lbs potatoes or yams = 1 lb bread
4 lbs rice or stockfish *or* 1 gal wheat = 1 gal oatmeal
1 qt calavances (chick peas or similar pulses) = 3 pts oatmeal *or*
    1 qt pease
1 pt oil = 1 lb butter
1 piece of pork (equivalent to 2 lbs) = 3 lbs beef
2 lbs flour + 8 oz currants = 1 piece of pork and pease
3 lbs mutton = 1 piece of beef *or* a piece of pork and pease
4 lbs flour = 1 piece of beef
2 lbs currants = 1 piece of beef
4 lbs raisins = 1 piece of beef

The officers normally ate their meals together, sitting at well-set tables either in the wardroom or the gunroom, and were waited on by crewmen or boys. The captain also had his own cook and a steward to wait on him. He usually ate alone, but he could also 'keep a table', which meant he could invite officers or guests to join him for dinner if he wished. The midshipmen had a separate mess in the cockpit, and were also entitled to servants, though fewer than the senior officers.

The men ate in groups known as 'messes', which were normally made up of four to twelve men. Each man would take it in turns to be 'mess cook', and bring meals to the rest of the mess on a weekly basis. At certain times of the day the mess cook would collect food rations from the purser or steward and bring them back to the mess or galley. When the ship's cook had boiled all the rations in a large copper, the mess cook would return, select the men's food and bring it back to the mess in a vessel known as a 'mess kid', a barrel with rope handles. As well as the cooked food, the men would eat the ship's biscuit, which was stored on the mess table in a bread barge. It was said that the men would have to tap the biscuit on the table to remove the weevils that would regularly infest the supply of dried bread.

Accompanying their meal, the men would drink a quantity of grog (one-part rum, three-parts water mixed with lemon juice and brown sugar), which was collected and distributed by the mess cook at his discretion, which meant he invariably gave himself a larger measure.

ORIGINS OF 'GROG'

The term 'grog' was first heard in the mid-eighteenth century, and originated from the nickname applied to an admiral stationed in Jamaica in 1740. Admiral Vernon, known in navy circles as 'Old Grogram' after the grogram boat cloak – grogram was a coarse silk cloth, often mixed with mohair or wool and stiffened with glue – which he wore, produced a new variation of drink in an attempt to reduce drunkenness and cases of scurvy among his men. Replacing the use of brandy with a local rum, he diluted the rum with four parts of water, and mixed it with brown sugar and lemon juice.

A SONG ABOUT GROG FROM AUBREY'S TIME

While sailing once our Captain, who was a jolly dog,
One day sarv'd out to every mess a double share of grog,
Ben Backstay he got tipsy all to his heart's content,
And being half-seas over, why overboard he went.
A shark was on his larboard, sharks don't for manners stand,
But grapple all that they come near like lawyer-sharks on land,
We threw out Ben some tackling of saving him in hopes,
But the shark he bit his head off so he couldn't see the ropes.
Without a head 'is ghost appears all on the briny lake,
He piped all hands ahoy and cried 'Lads, warning by me take,
By drinking I lost my life so lest my fate you meet,
Why never mix your liquor, lads, but always drink it straight.'
(Source: the Historical Maritime Society [www.hms.org.uk])

DRINKING LEVELS ON BOARD SHIP

Partly due to the generous ration of alcohol allowed to the men in the navy (the annual issue of beer per man was 365 gallons; a gallon a day on average) and as a consequence of the tough conditions in which they worked, drunkenness was a common feature of navy life among the men; officers were expected to remain sober at least while on duty. In fact the men could drink as much beer as they liked, since it was safer than drinking water, and not too strong. In addition they also received a half-pint rum ration per day, which was mixed with water to produce grog, which they drank with their dinner and supper.

The beer was brewed in the Victualling Board's own breweries, from October to the following spring. The finished product could not be well-preserved and usually did not keep for very long. When beer rations were finished, the men would receive substitute alcohol – 1 gallon of beer equalled a pint of wine or a half-pint of spirits. The wine, which would normally be watered down, was purchased in the Mediterranean by Victualling Board representatives, and was usually red, called 'black strap' by the men; white wine was known as 'Miss Taylor'.

The officers drank at least the same amount if not more than their men, as the more money they had, the more they were able to spend on a variety of different wines and spirits at each foreign port in which they docked.

Drunkenness was an inevitable by-product of the amount of alcohol available to the sailors. Punishments for drunken offences varied from captain to captain – some might put their men in chains until they had sobered up, whereas others were known to have flogged those men who had returned from the shore in no condition to reef or steer or fulfil their other nautical duties. The twenty-four hours after payday, on days when the ship was still anchored, would be particularly unproductive, as the men would freely spend their hard-earned money getting drunk ashore. For example, in January 1747/8, Rear Admiral Augustus Keppel found himself in an impossible situation as a consequence of his men's on-shore activities, writing to Admiral George Anson, 'We are now in a great hurry for sailing, and I in a sad pickle, with my whole ship's company drunk.'

TYPICAL BREAKFAST

The first meal of the day would be served up in the morning at about 8 o'clock.

Typical breakfast food for the men included skillygalee, which was a thin weak broth or oatmeal porridge boiled in fatty water; from the early nineteenth century onwards, a small amount of butter and sugar was added to the ingredients, to give a little extra flavour. The officers, however, would fare altogether better, as they could afford to supply their own food, which could include meat, fish, eggs and bread.

TYPICAL DINNER

Dinner was served at staggered intervals between midday and 4 p.m., and constituted the crew's main meal. The men and midshipmen would eat first at midday, followed by the officers in the wardroom an hour later, then the captain and lastly, on a flagship, the admiral.

The men would have a ration of bread and beer which they ate along with a portion of meat on four out of seven days (either beef or pork), and cheese and oatmeal on the remaining three days. Desserts included figgy-dowdy (crumbled ship's biscuit mixed with pork fat, plums, currants, rum and served with grog). The officers' dinners would vary, depending on the type of foodstuffs they had been able to purchase on-shore. In addition to the meals the men would eat, the officers might also consume fish, pies, a range of different meats, and for dessert they would have plum duff (a pudding made with flour, pork fat, sugar, raisins or currants) or spotted dog (a suet pudding made with flour, sugar, cinnamon, nutmeg, currants, eggs and milk), both of which would have been served with custard.

TYPICAL SUPPER

The men would eat the leftovers from dinner along with a pint of grog and some ship's biscuits. The officers might eat some soup, with some meat and bread, coffee and some leftover pudding.

NAUTICAL ORIGINS OF
COMMON PHRASES AND SAYINGS – 5

Garbled
The prohibited practice of mixing rubbish with the cargo was known as 'garbling'.

Groggy
In 1740, the British Admiral Edward Vernon (whose nickname was 'Old Grogram', from the cloak of grogram he wore) ordered that the sailors' daily ration of rum be diluted with water. The mixture was named 'grog', and drinking too much of it made men 'groggy'. (See ORIGINS OF 'GROG', p.56).

Gun – son of a gun
Occasionally children were born aboard British warships, and a convenient place for this was between guns on the gun deck. If a male child's father was not known, the newborn was entered in the ship's log as 'son of a gun'. (See WOMEN AT SEA, p.88).

Jib – the cut of (someone's or something's) jib
Warships would often have their triangular jib sails (the fore-and-aft sails at the bow of the ship, most of the other sails being horizontal squaresails) cut down to make them narrower so that they could 'maintain point' (i.e. heading) and not be blown off course. Upon sighting narrow foresails on a distant ship a captain, especially of a merchantman, might not like the cut of his jib (for it signified a warship, and possibly an enemy one) and would then have an opportunity to escape.

DISCIPLINE AND PUNISHMENT

Petty crime and anti-social behaviour was common in the navy, exacerbated by the close living and working conditions on board ship on voyages that could last months if not years. However, in the main, rowdy, insubordinate behaviour took place in port or on shore rather than on board, as every experienced seaman knew instinctively that at sea order had to be maintained for the safety of all. The green landsmen, seized by the press gangs or recruited from jails, had to learn the lesson of ship's discipline the hard way, often at the hands of their fellow sailors.

DEATH SENTENCE

The thirty-four Articles of War (1757) identified transgressions of naval law and laid down punishments that could be meted out by a court martial. The Articles were read aloud to the ship's company – many of whom were illiterate – at the ship's commissioning and once a month, usually on a Sunday.

There were at least seven crimes for which the death sentence was mandatory:

> Communicating with the enemy
> Failure to fight
> Failure to pursue enemy
> Sedition or mutiny
> Burning ship, boat or magazine
> Murder
> Buggery or sodomy of man or beast

The Articles also identified a further thirteen crimes for which the death sentence might be awarded but could be replaced by 'such punishment as a Court Martial shall think fit to inflict'.

COURTS MARTIAL

On the whole, ships' companies tried to avoid courts martial for the following reasons:

> The trial had to be presided over by the second-in-command of the squadron or port
>
> A minimum of five and maximum of thirteen post-captains or commanders had to attend
>
> A prosecuting officer, key witnesses and the accused had to be gathered, perhaps from different ships
>
> Trials could often last for several days, disrupting the navy's business (disastrous in times of war)

Owing to all these conditions, a court martial could take months to assemble. During this time, prisoners were kept in irons under permanent guard. Often transgressors were pardoned at their trials on the grounds that they had already suffered enough.

SEVERITY OF CRIMES

Despite the guidelines laid down in the Articles, the real crimes at sea were often identified rather differently by those living life on the ocean wave. Those regarded as the worst crimes were:

> Sodomy
> Murder
> Theft

Crimes unpopular with a ship's company because they added to the burden of others were:

> Neglect of work
> 'Skulking' below deck
> Uncleanliness

PUNISHMENTS

The captain more often than not acted as judge and jury and decided on the punishment according to the nature of the offence, the character of the culprit and any other extenuating circumstances. All crimes and punishments were meant to be recorded in the ship's log.

Flogging
This was the usual punishment administered in public for serious shipboard crimes. The offender would be tied in an upright spread-eagled position (or sometimes bent over a gun), perhaps with something in his mouth to bite on. He would then be lashed across the back and shoulders with a cat-o'-nine-tails, made of nine lengths of line knotted at intervals along their lengths. Officially a captain could award a maximum of twelve lashes, but this was regularly exceeded with the result that sailors were scarred for life. Some seamen were sentenced to the extremely severe punishment of being 'flogged around the fleet', where the offender was rowed to every ship in port to receive a specified number of lashes.

Running the gauntlet
This method was often used to punish thieves. The crew, each carrying a stick or piece of rope end, would line up in two columns. The perpetrator would have to pass between the two lines to receive a beating. (The Admiralty abolished this punishment in 1806.)

Caning or 'cobbing'
This was a less severe punishment than flogging and was often administered to and by midshipmen within the privacy of the gunroom.

Seized to the shrouds
This involved tying the culprit spread-eagled to the shrouds (ropes that extended from the masts to the sides of the ship).

Other punishments
An officer might be confined to quarters or ordered to stand a double watch. If a seaman held a position of responsibility he could be dis-rated. A common sailor could be put in irons, have his rum ration withdrawn, or be forced to clean the ship's 'heads' (latrines).

NAUTICAL ORIGINS OF
COMMON PHRASES AND SAYINGS – 6

Leeway
The lee side is the side of the ship sheltered from the wind, and the lee shore is a shore that is downwind of the ship. A ship without enough leeway therefore risks being driven on to the shore.

Line – to toe the line
When called to line up at attention on the deck, the ship's crew would form up with their toes touching a seam in the deck planking.

Loggerheads – to be at loggerheads
A loggerhead was a long-handled implement with an iron ball at one end. The ball end was heated and then used to seal the pitch in deck seams, and the expression probably originated because it was occasionally used as a weapon by quarrelling crewmen.

Offing – to be in the offing
The offing is the more distant part of the sea as seen from land; also used to mean the distance which, for safety, a ship kept from land – hence, a good distance from shore, and thus barely visible from land. The much-loved English folk song 'Blow The Wind Southerly' includes the line 'They told me last night there were ships in the offing', in other words, ships approaching the harbour and safety.

Overbearing
To overbear means to sail downwind directly at another (usually enemy) ship, thus, when close enough, diverting the wind from her sails. Hence also the expression 'to take the wind from someone's sails'.

Overwhelm
In nautical terms, to be overwhelmed meant to capsize or sink, often as the result of being swamped by a heavy sea.

ENTERTAINMENT AND RECREATION ABOARD A MAN-OF-WAR

The seamen and officers of Nelson's navy were resourceful and creative in entertaining themselves during their 'leisure' hours. While the officers benefited from the three watch system, the demands of the watch left very little free time to be filled by the men in pastimes and leisurely pursuits. Naval tradition and the proclivities of the captain dictated the kinds of hobbies and other activities that the men might pursue, and the absence of formal shore leave meant that the seamen were forced to occupy themselves in any way they could. Such 'entertainment' might have included:

Yarning
The telling of tall tales of bravery and adventure, ghost stories and fables.

Skylarking
The unfettered athletic exercise greatly enjoyed by boys and young men. It involved racing up and playing in the rigging.

Scrimshaw
Scrimshaw work was the carving of ornaments and other decorative objects from those materials most available at sea; ivory, the jawbones or teeth of whales, tusks of walruses and the vertebrae of any sea mammal. In skilled hands the work could be very intricate indeed; as many sailors had been artisans on shore, or were trained in a trade such as shoemaking or hatmaking, the men often liked to keep up their skills in their spare time.

Forbitters
These were songs sung around the forecastle, telling of past victories and glories and as accolades to the bravery or triumphs of the greatest vessels and their masters. They contrasted with shanties, which were traditionally work songs sung to a rhythm to facilitate a task. Some forbitters were satirical and many ribald or obscene. They represented a harmless way for the men to express both their creativity and air their grievances. Other songs were sentimental, airing the men's longings for home and loved ones. (See p.70)

Music and dancing
The ship's company would often include a fiddler and a marine fifer and many men would bring instruments aboard, or make them in their spare time. The dancing of jigs and hornpipes was permitted and no doubt much enjoyed, particularly under the influence of grog.

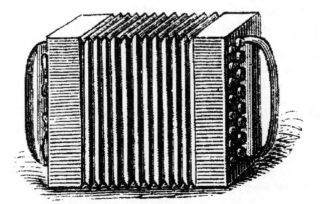

Embroidery

Many young men spent time decorating their clothes with ribbons sewn into the seams of their shirts and trousers or with embroidery and crewel work. The foretopmen were often the youngest and most decorated in the navy.

Practical jokes

The ship's company would often include a number of children, boys as young as six years old. While skylarking was their preferred game playing practical jokes came a good second.

Grinning

These curious face-pulling competitions were very popular. A horse collar was worn around the neck to frame the hideous faces being pulled and prizes were awarded to the winners.

Gambling and Dicing

Although the Articles of War expressly forbade gambling and dicing, many, particularly the officers, indulged in them covertly.

DIVERSIONS

Drinking

The clichéd maritime leisure pursuit, nevertheless it was very true that sailors were particularly heavy drinkers. In part through boredom, and in part through the quantities of alcohol allocated to each man (see pp.57-8), drinking was a permitted pastime on board a Royal Navy vessel. However, it has been estimated that drunkenness was the most common cause of flogging. On a more positive note, drinking alcohol was often more healthy than drinking the ship's water.

Tobacco

This could be bought from the purser or in port, but it was forbidden to smoke below desks, which is why chewing tobacco became popular.

Sex

Despite the men being confined to ship (primarily through the officers' fear of desertion), women were allowed on board, and to remain if the ship was in port for several days. The obvious would follow, though (through circumstance) largely conducted with no thought as to privacy or decency. The ship's surgeon would often report an increased number of gonorrhoea and syphilis cases once the vessel returned to open waters. Homosexuality was punishable by death but was not unknown on board ship; however, most of the contemporary reports by seamen make no mention of it.

Crossing the Line

Crossing the Equator provided a peculiarly theatrical entertainment that all aboard could appreciate. Those who had never crossed before would be brought before 'King Neptune' and a bizarre entourage of nymphs and bears. King Neptune's court was held around a large canvas bath on the forecastle, and the 'first-timers' would be asked if they had travelled this way before, and forced to pay their tribute. Some would pay a fine but others would be greased or tarred, then shaved and ducked into the sailor's bathing tub.

OFFICERS' ENTERTAINMENT

Officers amused themselves much as they would on land during their longer hours of leisure. Entertaining, where the provision of a competent cook could afford officers the opportunity to display their possessions and the offering of lavish hospitality, formed a large part of 'society' aboard ship. Officers might also take the opportunity to practise their skills with swords and small arms, which also could lead to the challenging of each other over real or imagined matters of honour. An officer might pursue a talent for literature or painting, and these skills could be pressed into service in recording the detail of encounters with other ships or of lands visited, or of their flora and fauna.

The indiscriminate press-ganging of 'volunteers' often produced people of extraordinary talents among the ship's company. Actors and circus performers, dancers and musicians could be persuaded to perform plays, farces and reviews. When in port a captain might bring on board any manner of local entertainers, troupes of dancers and musicians to amuse and entertain the men.

A FORBITTER – 'BOLD NELSON'S PRAISE'

Bold Nelson's praise I am going to sing,
(Not forgetting our glorious King)
He always did good tidings bring,
For he was a bold commander.
There was Sydney Smith and Duncan too,
Lord Howe and all the glorious crew;
They were the men that were true blue.
Full of care, yet I swear
None with Nelson could compare,
Not even Alexander.

Bold Buonaparte he threaten'd war,
A man who fear'd not wound nor scar,
But still he lost at Trafalgar
Where Britain was victorious.
Lord Nelson's actions made him quake,
And all French pow'rs he made to shake;
He said his king he'd ne'er forsake.
These last words thus he spake,
Stand true, my lads, like hearts of oak,
And the battle shall be glorious.

Lord Nelson bold, though threaten'd wide,
And many a time he had been tried,
He fought like a hero till he died
Amid the battle gory.
But the day was won, their line was broke,
While all around was lost in smoke,
And Nelson he got his death-stroke,
That's the man for old England!
He faced his foe with his sword in hand
And he lived and he died in his glory.

RECRUITMENT

During the eighteenth century, the Royal Navy recruited by ship, not by service; in other words, the seamen (not commissioned officers) were assigned to a vessel or they were not employed at all. Volunteers would work until such time that they were discharged after a ship had completed its mission, or if chosen to remain could sail again with their current ship. In this regard they were very much members of the ship's company and could join a vessel as opportunity or preference allowed. In peacetime the Royal Navy had sufficient men in those who were already able seamen or skilled in their trades, and if necessary, trained manpower could easily be drawn from the merchant service. Most seamen learned their trade from boyhood, joining a ship often as young as eight years old. It was important for potential seamen to begin learning their trade early if they were to exercise their skills at the peak of their fitness – the majority of the ship's complement would be in their early twenties. While it may be hard to comprehend why a life in the navy was such an attractive proposition to some, it must be remembered that most people never travelled beyond the borders of their own town, let alone country. The opportunity to sail to distant lands in the company of one's peers, with the provision of (relatively) decent food and treatment, while training for a trade that provided a good income and even a pension, would have appeared very attractive for some.

During a period of war, such as the time in which Aubrey's experiences are set, it became necessary for the Royal Navy to find extra seamen. Their first recourse was to offer incentives to attract volunteers; those

aboard a merchant vessel, at the mercy of enemy fleets and privateers, might have found the £70 bounty tempting, particularly for the better conditions in the King's service.

The total sums paid by the Admiralty to all volunteers for each year between 1755 and 1762 – rather earlier than Aubrey's time, but still applying in many cases – were as follows:

1755	£16,800 30s 0d
1756	£16,335 10s 0d
1757	£11,676 10s 0d
1758	£9,406 0s 0d
1759	£12,767 10s 0d
1760	£8,868 0s 0d
1761	£4,312 10s 0d
1762	£16,121 10s 0d (including arrears)

The Royal Navy was able to buy food and provisions in bulk at keener prices and provided better medical services as well as a pension. However, when it became impossible to meet its recruitment needs through volunteers alone, the infamous Impress Service, or 'press gangs', provided men by other means.

PRESS GANGS

Under the leadership of a lieutenant, the gangs were warranted to press into service seamen from incoming ships, watermen and seafarers on land. They could not press landsmen with no experience of the sea, and indeed, it was not to their advantage to do so. The pay and expenses for a lieutenant (he would receive a pound for each man pressed) and his men in a press gang could easily exceed that which he could earn aboard ship, which was why they 'recruited' with such vigour. A gang would set up a rendezvous base at an inn, usually in a coastal town, and round up seamen who were hiding ashore. Along with any volunteers, they would be held in a room, and eventually distributed among the ships. A volunteer was free to choose his ship either by reputation or because he had friends on board, but a pressed man would have to go where he was sent. By claiming a full complement a captain could technically refuse a pressed man, if the seaman lacked experience or was known to be troublesome. Pressing on land was not easy. A local authority had to

stamp warrants, and magistrates and mayors could and did oppose this if it meant losing votes or if they were trying to limit civil disturbance that might arise in opposition to the press.

By far the most frequent and successful way of recruiting experienced seamen was at sea, where the gangs could recruit both volunteers and pressed men from merchant ships. Smugglers were a popular choice for the gangs because they had excellent seamanship skills and were willing to avoid prosecution by joining a King's ship. Magistrates were able to empty debtors' prisons by allowing the navy to discharge the debts and authorizing the debtors to be pressed into service. Pressed men had no right of leave and ships that had completed their commission were often 'turned-over' at sea and their crews distributed among other ships. By 1793 all British seamen or mariners were liable to be pressed unless they were exempt. Theoretically, whalers, mates on merchant ships, colliers, sailmakers and so on, as well as apprentices, were protected from the press, and there was a great trade in forging apprentices' indentures and other protective documents as the merchant service attempted to keep its ships manned. The available records make it almost impossible to know how many of the navy's recruits were volunteers and how many were pressed, but in the absence of conscription the Impress Service remained a vital means of manning the ships. Even so, the demand for experienced seamen far exceeded the supply. Keeping an experienced crew together was the main aim of the captain, and a wise captain would run as happy a ship as possible, keeping his crew through the lure of prize money, good conditions and glory. Influence remained an important part of the officer's armoury.

NAUTICAL ORIGINS OF
COMMON PHRASES AND SAYINGS – 7

Pipe down
'Lights out' and 'Silence' were signalled by the last call of the bosun's pipe at the end of the day.

Pooped
To be pooped originally meant to be swamped by a heavy following sea. The poop deck, found only in the larger ships, is a small deck at the aftermost end of the quarterdeck, i.e. at the stern.

Ropes – to know the ropes
There were miles and miles of cordage in the rigging of a square-rigged ship. It took an experienced seaman to know the position and function of all the ropes, halyards, stays, sheets, and so on.

Rummage sale
From the French *arrumage* meaning ship's cargo. Damaged cargo was sold off at reduced prices at a rummage sale.

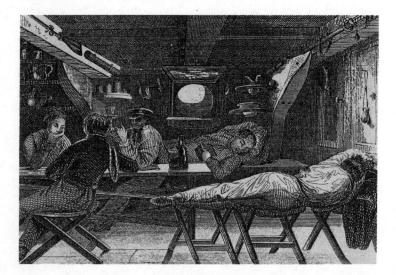

MEDICAL MATTERS ON BOARD SHIP

Surgeons received a warrant from the Navy Board, having usually learned their trade before going to sea, often by apprenticeship rather than by acquiring a medical degree, although towards the end of the eighteenth century, many more surgeons with degrees from new medical schools in Glasgow and Edinburgh joined the naval ranks, which greatly improved the quality of medical care on board naval vessels.

Once appointed to a ship, they served as surgeon's mates (renamed 'assistant surgeons' in 1805) for a time before being granted the rank of surgeon. On board they served as physicians as well as surgeons proper, with responsibility for all the sick, injured and wounded, regardless of rank.

Most patients would visit the surgeons in the area that became known as a 'sick bay' or 'sick berth', usually a small area closed off by canvas or partitions, which had enough space to accommodate a few ailing men, as well as the surgeon's desk, medical equipment and medication.

On a daily basis, the surgeon was responsible for treating every conceivable medical complaint, from the everyday maladies of toothache and seasickness, to boils and abscesses. Physical injuries among the seamen were also common, including fractures caused by falls or concussion caused by the banging of heads on low deck beams or by falling objects. Internal ruptures or hernias were also often sustained by the men as a consequence of the daily lifting and lowering of heavy casks and other weighty objects.

Due to the numbers of men living together in conditions that were often quite cramped, disease tended to spread quickly, from influenza, typhus and consumption, to malaria, cholera and yellow fever in more tropical climes. Bouts of gonorrhoea and syphilis were also common after sailors had spent a period of time on land. Scurvy was a disease rife among the men at sea, which spread aboard ships when supplies of fresh fruit and vegetables ran out, and could not always be replaced swiftly. This left the sailors with a much reduced source of vital vitamins, and could result in scurvy, the symptoms of which included bleeding gums, anaemia, a general lack of energy and exhaustion. When the seriousness of the disease was realized, steps were taken to treat the afflicted, but it was not until the mid-eighteenth century that a breakthrough came, when Scottish naval surgeon James Lind began having success when treating scurvy-ridden sailors with lemons and oranges. By 1795 the Royal Navy had begun to distribute regular rations of lime juice on long voyages (which led to the 'limeys' nickname given to British sailors) to keep the disease at bay.

Infection or 'sepsis' was also a major cause of death, even from just a minor cut to the hand. If a crush injury or a bullet wound was serious enough to lead to amputation, the limb was duly severed and the arteries and blood vessels were tied off with ligatures and left to drop away from the stump after a certain length of time, which meant the exposed area was particularly prone to infection. Even if a man survived the initial operation, there was always a strong possibility of death if post-operative infection set in and took hold, causing the skin to become inflamed, perhaps developing into gangrene or tetanus, at the very worst. Tissue and skin that became gangrenous could be cut away during follow-up surgery, but tetanus invariably turned into lockjaw, and the treatment (including twice-daily warm baths and the oral consumption of opium grains) was slow-working and far from effective.

SUMMARY OF ROYAL NAVY FATALITIES FOR 1810

Cause of death	Numbers	Percentage
Disease	2,592	50
Accident	1,630	31.5
Wreck, fire, explosion	530	10.2
Killed in action by enemy	281	5.4
Died of battle wounds	150	2.9
All causes	*5,183*	*100*

In action, the surgeons usually took post in the orlop (lowest) deck, and dealt with wounded and injured men in the order in which they arrived, rather than according to the severity of their injuries; as a result, they became extremely adept at assessing wounds and even performing major

surgery, in cramped and often chaotic conditions, extremely quickly, and it was by no means uncommon for an amputation to be performed in a few minutes, which was vital for the patient's survival from shock, at a time when anaesthetics had yet to be properly developed. Restricted to using only their own medication and equipment until 1804, the surgeons would be aided by the 'loblolly' men, unskilled assistants who worked with them particularly during surgical procedures. Without proper pain relief or anaesthesia, it was often the case that men who had been so badly injured they were beyond saving, would be dropped overboard by their able-bodied shipmates as an act of mercy.

During firefights between opposing vessels, the men on board were most likely to be injured by flying splinters, especially those that resulted from the impact of a cannon ball from an enemy ship, which produced far more deaths or injuries than being hit by the ball itself.

Other common injuries during battle were burns of varying degrees. Fever and shock would often accompany the physical burn damage, as well as the inevitable onset of infection, which the surgeon would treat by giving the patient opiates, which were taken orally.

A more unusual injury associated with the firing of cannon was known as 'wind of ball' by naval surgeons of the eighteenth and nineteenth century. When a cannon ball came within close proximity of a seaman on its speeding course, it might leave no physical wounds, but could still cause immediate death. If it passed close to the stomach, damage was likely to be fatal, but if the cannon ball went past the head, death would rarely result. The cause of death arising from 'wind of ball' was beyond the comprehension of naval surgeons at that time, but one must assume that the force of its flight must have caused internal injuries to those who narrowly avoided direct collision on its course.

As well as the hands-on activities involved in treating members of the crew, it was also the surgeon's responsibility to ensure that the ship was kept clean – both the men on board and the vessel's numerous decks and rooms. The sick-bay in particular was regularly fumigated, normally by burning sulphur (brimstone). The surgeons also made sure that the ventilating machines which provided the lower decks with fresh air were fully functional.

NAVAL MEDICAL TRIVIA

From 1795 to 1805, those men dying from disease and individual accidents accounted for 82 per cent of the Royal Navy's losses during the naval warfare with France. Major accidents, for example sinking, accounted for 12 per cent, with the remaining 6 per cent being deaths occurring in battle.

Instances of insanity were thought to affect one in every thousand seamen, which was a rate that was seven times higher than the population on land. Navy doctors formed the strong opinion that most cases of madness were caused by head injuries that were usually sustained when the sailor was in a state of drunkenness.

TYPICAL TREATMENTS

Burns
Various treatments would be applied by the surgeon to the injured parts after cleaning, including vinegar compresses, linseed oil, olive oil (which kept the skin soft during the healing process) and lime water.

Hernias
These were treated by manipulating the displaced bit of intestine back into the abdominal cavity, and a truss was supplied to ensure the intestine stayed in place.

Bad teeth
In the absence of proper dental knowledge, surgeons would have to pull problem teeth from their patient's mouth, using gripping implements such as a turnkey.

Open wounds
Arteries were tied off to stop the flow of blood, foreign bodies were removed from the wound if necessary, and the affected area of skin was cleaned, sometimes using nitrate solutions to control inflammation; dressings were changed as regularly as possible to reduce inflammation and pus seepage.

Heavy bleeding
To prevent massive blood loss, a canvas tourniquet was applied to the damaged area, and a screw, which was connected to a brass plate placed over the ruptured artery, would be turned and tightened to compress the injury and stem the flow of blood. Compression bandages would then be placed over the wound, and surgery would doubtless follow.

NAUTICAL ORIGINS OF
COMMON PHRASES AND SAYINGS – 8

Sails – taking the wind out of someone's sails
To sail close to another ship in such a way and from such a direction as to steal or divert wind from her sails.

Scuttlebutt
The scuttlebutt was a barrel of drinking water set on deck for all to use; it tended to be the place where the ship's gossip was exchanged.

Service – to press into service
Impressment, carried out by press gangs (see pp.72-3), was one of the means by which the navy filled its ships' crew quotas – in essence, by kidnapping men and forcing them into service.

Shakes – no great shakes
Empty casks were 'shaken' (taken apart) so the pieces, called shakes, could be stored in as small a space as possible. These shakes had very little value.

Skyscraper
The small triangular sail above the skysail used to maximize the benefit of a light wind.

Slate – to start over with a clean slate
The watch keeper would record the speeds, distances, headings and tacks during the watch on a slate. If there were no problems during the watch, the slate would be wiped clean so that the new watch could start over with a clean slate.

Slush fund
Fat was obtained by boiling or scraping the empty barrels in which salted meat had been stored. This 'slush' was often sold to the purser or ashore by the ship's cook, for himself or the crew. The money that resulted became known as a slush fund.

Square meal
Hot meals were served on square wooden platters.

COST OF HMS *VICTORY*

2,000 oak trees were used in her construction – equivalent to 60 acres of forest. Final cost was £63,176, which is equivalent to over £50 million ($80 million) today.

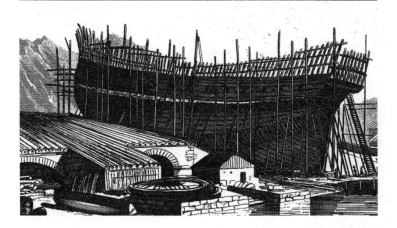

SOME ROYAL NAVY SHIPYARDS IN AUBREY'S DAY

Buckler's Hard, Hampshire
Frindsbury, Kent
Dover, Kent
Chatham, Kent
Ipswich, Suffolk
Leith, Edinburgh
Brightlingsea, Essex
Kingston-upon-Hull, Yorkshire
Pembroke, Pembrokeshire
Rochester, Kent
Topsham, Devon
Jamaica

THE DUTIES OF THE ROYAL NAVY

To protect Britain from invasion
To blockade enemy fleets and ports
To convoy British merchant trading ships, and those foreign vessels bringing cargo between Britain and its trading partners
To cruise, maintaining a Royal Navy presence, deterring the movement of enemy warships and merchant vessels
To supply and support the British army in its overseas operations

SELECTED ARTICLES OF WAR

The Articles of War were Royal Navy rules and regulations governing the behaviour of officers and seamen. They were to be read once a month to the entire crew.

Article One
All commanders, captains, and officers, in or belonging to any of His Majesty's ships or vessels of war, shall cause the public worship of Almighty God, according to the liturgy of the Church of England established by law, to be solemnly, orderly and reverently performed in their respective ships; and shall take care that prayers and preaching, by the chaplains in holy orders of the respective ships, be performed diligently; and that the Lord's day be observed according to law.

Article Five
If any letter or message from any enemy or rebel, be conveyed to any officer, mariner, or soldier or other in the fleet, and the said officer, mariner, or soldier, or other as aforesaid, shall not, within twelve hours, having opportunity so to do, acquaint his superior or a commanding

officer, or if any superior officer being acquainted therewith, shall not in convenient time reveal the same to the commander in chief of the squadron, every such person so offending, and being convicted thereof by the sentence of the court martial, shall be punished with death, or such other punishment as the nature and degree of the offence shall deserve, and the court martial shall impose.

Article Nine
If any ship or vessel be taken as prize, none of the officers, mariners, or other persons on board her, shall be stripped of their clothes, or in any sort pillaged, beaten, or evil-intreated, upon the pain that the person or persons so offending, shall be liable to such punishment as a court martial shall think fit to inflict.

Article Thirteen
Every person in the fleet, who through cowardice, negligence, or disaffection, shall forbear to pursue the chase of any enemy, pirate or rebel, beaten or flying; or shall not relieve or assist a known friend in view to the utmost of his power; being convicted of any such offence by the sentence of a court martial, shall suffer death.

Article Twenty-Two
If any officer, mariner, soldier or other person in the fleet, shall strike any of his superior officers, or draw, or offer to draw, or lift up any weapon against him, being in the execution of his office, on any pretence whatsoever, every such person being convicted of any such offence, by the sentence of a court martial, shall suffer death; and if any officer, mariner, soldier or other person in the fleet, shall presume to quarrel with any of his superior officers, being in the execution of his office, or shall disobey any lawful command of any of his superior officers; every such person being convicted of any such offence, by the sentence of a court martial, shall suffer death, or such other punishment, as shall, according to the nature and degree of his offence, be inflicted upon him by the sentence of a court martial.

Article Twenty-Nine
If any person in the fleet shall commit the unnatural and detestable sin of buggery and sodomy with man or beast, he shall be punished with death by the sentence of a court martial.

ROYAL NAVY TOASTS

The midshipman, or the newest officer, would propose the official Royal Navy toasts in the mess room each day after dinner. For each day of the week, the toasts would be:

Monday – 'For our ships at sea'
Tuesday – 'For our men'
Wednesday – 'For ourselves (as no-one else is likely to concern themselves with our welfare)'
Thursday – 'A bloody war or a sickly season'
Friday – 'A willing foe and sea room'
Saturday – 'Sweethearts and wives (may they never meet)'
Sunday – 'Absent friends'

FOREIGN NATIONALS SERVING ON HMS *VICTORY* AT THE BATTLE OF TRAFALGAR

22 Americans
7 Dutch
6 Swedes
4 Italians
4 Maltese
3 French (all volunteers)
3 Norwegians
3 Germans
2 Swiss
2 Portuguese
2 Danes
2 Indians
1 Russian
1 African
9 'from the West Indian islands'

FIRST LORDS OF THE ADMIRALTY, 1788–1815

John Pitt, 2nd Earl of Chatham	16 Jul 1788 – 19 Dec 1794
George John Spencer	19 Dec 1794 – 19 Feb 1801
Admiral John Jervis, 1st Earl of St Vincent	19 Feb 1801 – 15 May 1804
Henry Dundas, 1st Viscount Melville	15 May 1804 – 2 May 1805
Admiral Charles Middleton, Lord Barham	2 May 1805 – 10 Feb 1806
Hon. Charles Grey, Viscount Howick	10 Feb 1806 – 29 Sept 1806
Thomas Grenville	29 Sept 1806 – 6 Apr 1807
Henry Phipps, 3rd Lord Mulgrave	6 Apr 1807 – 4 May 1810
Charles Philip Yorke	4 May 1810 – 25 Mar 1812
Robert Saunders Dundas, 2nd Viscount Melville	25 Mar 1812 – 2 May 1827

NAUTICAL ORIGINS OF
COMMON PHRASES AND SAYINGS – 9

Touch and go
When, in shallow water or over shoals, the ship's keel touches or brushes the bottom but does not become grounded, leaving the vessel able to move off again.

Two-six
This expression, often used as a command for others to lift a heavy object in unison, originated with a ship's gun crew. With the gun reloaded, the gun captain would call 'Two, Six – ho!', the command for the No. 2 and No. 6 members of the crew to heave on the side tackles to run the gun out again.

Weather – to be under the weather
A crewman standing watch on the weather (the windward, as opposed to the lee) side of the bow will be subject to the constant beating of the sea, and thus 'under the weather'.

Windfall
Wind blowing from off a lee shore (see Leeway, p.65), against the general direction of the wind. Encountering a windfall (which often occurred from mountainous coastlines) might win a ship more leeway – hence the word's meaning as a sudden and unexpected piece of luck.

SIGNALS

During the eighteenth century the issue of ship-to-ship communication was a concern for every commander. The signal code used by the Royal Navy had been devised by Admiral Lord Howe in 1790. Each commander was issued with a copy of *Fighting Instructions for His Majesty's Fleet*, in which were printed the fourteen designated signal pennants: those representing numbers one to nine, another for zero, a flag for 'repeater', and the final three 'control' flags denoting 'preparative', 'finishing' and 'affirmative'. In combination almost 260 messages could be signalled, and with certain modifications and improvements made in 1799, this number increased to approximately 340, which were collected in the Admiralty's *Signal Book for Ships of War*. While signalling was incredibly useful and supplemented the other methods of communication, such as face-to-face conferences, conveying written orders by boat and the use of a megaphone (when vessels were in close proximity), it still presented difficulties in conveying signals relating to unforeseen circumstances. Naturally, such eventualities were an inevitability of wartime engagements.

In 1800 an ingenious refinement was made to this basic system by Admiral Sir Home Popham. Popham created the world's first alphabetic flag system; flags 1 to 9 represented A to J, and the rest of the alphabet was made up through two-flag hoists. Crucially, his system also included a numbered dictionary of predefined words and phrases, and offered the facility to spell out words not represented in the book. Fundamentally, this allowed complex messages to be sent relatively quickly, and gave a flexibility to the messages that could be sent. Successful signalling also relied on reading the flags in the right order, which depended on which masts the pennants were hoisted. A useful example is given by reading the famous 'England expects' message issued by Nelson before Trafalgar.

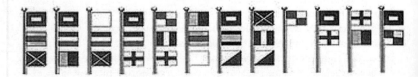

The message would be read in the following order:

1. Read down the mainmast
2. Read down the foremast
3. Read down the mizzen mast
4. Read down the peak, or gaff
5. Read down the starboard side of the mainmast
6. Read down the port side of the mainmast
7. Read down the starboard side of the foremast
8. Read down the port side of the foremast
9. Read down the starboard side of the mizzen mast
10. Read down the port side of the mizzen mast

Reading the flags in this order, the message appeared as follows:

Mainmast – '2', '5', '3' – 'ENGLAND', followed by
Mainmast – '2', '6', '9' – 'EXPECTS'
Foremast – '8', '6', '3' – 'THAT' followed by
Foremast – '2', '6', '1' – 'EVERY'
Mizzen mast – '4', '7', '1' – 'MAN'
Gaff – '9', '5', '8' – 'WILL'
Mainmast, starboard side – '2', '2', '0' – 'DO'
Mainmast, port side – '3', '7', '0' – 'HIS'
Foremast, starboard side – '4'– 'D'
Foremast, port side – '2', '1' – 'U'
Mizzen mast, starboard side – '1', '9' – 'T'
Mizzen mast, port side – '2', '4' – 'Y'

The signal did not 'say' exactly what Nelson first intended. When given 'Nelson confides that every man will do his duty,' Nelson's signal officer, Lieutenant Pasco, asked if he could replace 'Nelson' with 'England' and substitute 'expects' for 'confides' because it would mean spelling those words out. Nelson is said to have replied, 'That will do, Pasco, make it directly.'

By positioning frigates at the extremity of signalling range, captains could receive prior warning of approaching enemy fleets; the range of this signalling could be increased by using one or more vessels in between as relays, with the only limitation being the power of the telescopes and the vigilance of the lookouts. At night a system of guns, lights and flares could be used to send over seventy predefined messages; twenty signals could be made and understood in foggy conditions.

Successive signal-book additions contained the same basic flag designs, but the numbers assigned to them varied in each edition. If the enemy managed to break their signal code by observing Royal Navy ships in action, this tactic ensured that in time the signals would change and therefore they would need deciphering again. To guard against the signal book being captured by a boarding party, heavy lead plates were bolted to the covers so that a defeated captain could throw it overboard, knowing that it would sink to the bottom.

Two night and fog signals
Four lights in a square, three guns fired slowly – 'alter course to starboard'. Two guns fired in quick succession, repeated thirty seconds later, answered by the ringing of bells – 'tack'.

WOMEN AT SEA

As early as 1587 a written statute existed that strictly prohibited women on board ship, but it is clear that this ruling was often ignored. When a ship came into port the Admiralty extended temporary visitors' rights to the wives of the seamen on board, which also gave a great boost to the local prostitution trade, for prostitutes were often brought aboard masquerading as wives. However, at an officer's invitation, women were legitimately allowed on board, and this privilege was often extended to captains' wives, and occasionally to those of warrant officers, too. Their presence was often invaluable during battle, where they would assist the surgeon in his ministrations, or carry cartridges and shot for the gunners, as well as relay news of the battle situation to the sailors below decks. Records indicate that a number of women were present at the Battle of the Nile, and that they petitioned for the right to be awarded commendations for their actions. However, perhaps the most remarkable group of women who served aboard Royal Navy vessels were those who disguised themselves as men. The apocryphal story of 'William Brown' is a noteworthy example; following eleven years of service Brown was revealed to be a woman, and her abilities as a sailor were so admired that she was promoted to captain of the forecastle.

MISCELLANEOUS WEEKLY DUTIES ABOARD THE HMS *BELLEROPHON*

Monday
Wash clothes; gunnery exercises; repair faulty gun parts

Tuesday
Scrub the hammocks; musket exercise by the marines; air the bedding

Wednesday
Scrub the boat sails; exercise in reefing and furling the sails

Thursday
The men to wash themselves; mend clothing; deck inspection by the master at arms

Friday
Gun exercises at the great guns; wash clothes

Saturday
Decks cleaned

Sunday
Clean hammocks put up; church services; free time in the afternoon

MUTINY

The act of mutiny, either by an individual or collectively by a ship's crew, was defined as open revolt against one's superiors. Two great mutinies shook the Royal Navy in 1797, namely the Spithead and the Nore mutinies. At the former, an anchorage in the east Solent between England and the Isle of Wight, prior to their departure on the March cruise the men of the Channel Fleet had expressed their grievances about pay and conditions. They were assured that on their return the matter would have been dealt with – upon being ordered to depart for their next tour of duty in April, however, and finding that their concerns had not been addressed, they refused to sail. There had been no increase in wages for over one hundred and fifty years, while the real cost of living in that time had increased by 30 per cent. There were also complaints about the treatment of the sick, lack of fresh vegetables, and the embezzlement of the comforts they had been given to improve their quality of life. This was a justified and well-conceived mutiny, and the mutineers were treated with respect, their insurrection carried out through the withholding of labour rather than aggressive confrontation. In due course the mutineers' requirements were met without reprisal.

The mutiny at the Nore was a far less peaceable action. Perhaps stirred up by infiltrating French agents, and the successful mutiny by the mariners at Spithead, it was led by Richard Parker of HMS *Sandwich*. The mutineers demanded more shore leave, changes to the Articles of War, the removal of some unpopular officers, and the fairer distribution of prize money. They occupied the majority of the vessels at Nore port and used them in an attempted blockade of London, but capitulated when other vessels were brought against them and shore batteries erected in haste to threaten the mutineers from land. Parker gave himself up, and was hanged along with twenty-four of his fellow conspirators.

One of the most notorious mutinies in the Royal Navy occurred in 1797 in the West Indies, aboard the frigate *Hermione*. It was captained by the brutal Hugh Pigot, who was infamous for his draconian discipline and harsh punishments. Dissatisfied with the work of his crew, he threatened to flog the last crew members to make it down from the rigging. As a consequence, two seamen panicked and fell to their deaths; when Pigot ordered the bodies to be tossed into the sea without ceremony, the *Hermione*'s hard-pressed crew finally snapped, killing Pigot and eight other officers, and handing the vessel over to the Spanish. In *The Far Side of the World*, Aubrey takes prisoner a number of *Hermione* mutineers, and in *The Reverse of the Medal* is present at their court-martial, to his distaste, reflecting that he would very likely have taken part in the mutiny himself had he been present. In 1799, the *Hermione* was captured back by HMS *Surprise*; the *Surprise* is Aubrey's favourite vessel, although in O'Brian's novels it has a different history from its real-life counterpart. *Blue at the Mizzen* concludes with Aubrey on board HMS *Surprise*, ready finally to raise his flag as admiral.

BELLS TOLLED TO MARK THE HOUR

> Start of the afternoon watch
> Twelve o'clock – eight bells
> Twelve-thirty – one bell
> One o'clock – two bells
> One-thirty – three bells
> Two o'clock – four bells
> Two-thirty – five bells
> Three o'clock – six bells
> Three-thirty – seven bells
> Four o'clock – eight bells

Following this, the cycle was repeated for each watch.

HEATING, VENTILATION, LIGHTING

The masses of men aboard the average man-of-war meant that heating was scarcely necessary, even in the higher latitudes. Portable stoves were used to dry the ship when it was empty, rather than heat the seamen. For ventilation, bellows were used to pump out the air below decks, and this task had to be kept up continually, particularly in summer. However, on the lower decks clothing and bedding were perpetually damp which caused rheumatism and exacerbated the damage of the sailors' exposure to cold. Candles were the chief source of light and for obvious reasons were kept in lanterns. They were extinguished in the evening to minimize the fire hazard, and this was strictly enforced by the master at arms.

HAMMOCKS

Official allocation of sleeping space was 14 inches per seaman, or 28 inches for a petty officer, but a two-watch system (where only half the crew were asleep at one time) meant that in reality each man had twice that. The hammocks were 6 feet (1.83m) x 3 feet (0.91m), made of cloth, and contained a mattress, bedding, pillow and coverlet. The hammocks were the property of the Navy Board, but each man either brought the bedding from shore, or acquired it from the ship's purser.

DISASTERS AND HAZARDS AT SEA

It may be surprising to read that the loss of life through combat with the enemy was by far the most insignificant factor in naval mortality.

Estimated Fatal Casualties in the Royal Navy 1793-1815

Cause of Death	Number	Percentage
Individual, non-combat (disease and personal accidents)	84,440	81.5

Collective, non-combat (foundering, shipwreck, fire, explosion)	12,680	12.2
Enemy action	6,540	6.3
TOTAL	103,660	100

(*Source: O'Neill,* Patrick O'Brian's Navy)

To put these figures in perspective, it must be held in mind that the British people in the nineteenth century suffered from the ravages of disease and deprivation to a far greater extent than its population does today. Doctors often hindered rather than helped, science was ignorant of many of the true causes of disease, or attributed erroneous origins to common ailments, and the general populace's adherence to a sanitary lifestyle was infrequent at best.

The hazards of working aboard ship day and night, through every conceivable weather condition, often at great heights and involving heavy weights and dangerous rigging meant that falls, slips, strains, broken bones, concussion and amputations were all a very real possibility. Falling from the rigging was often fatal, especially if the crewman hit the deck. Falling overboard was preferable as long as the sailor could be reached in time. However, as lifeboats were primitive and life jackets non-existent, and because there were no attempts to train seamen to swim, many of these unfortunate men could not survive long enough for any help to reach them.

Despite their great size and sturdy construction, the ships of the Georgian Royal Navy were dependent on the wind, and often at the mercy of poor maps and uncharted waters. Many vessels ran aground on reefs, collided with other vessels, or foundered in storms. The debris of shipwrecks that had accumulated over the years and settled on the seabed destroyed many ships, particularly those that tended to stay close to land, such as sloops and brigs. The Royal Navy's greatest loss was of the *St George* and the *Defence* in 1811 (the former was Nelson's flagship at the first Battle of Copenhagen); returning to England they were caught in a hurricane on the Danish coast and destroyed on the rocks. Over one thousand two hundred men were lost. Prior to the period in question, but highlighting the dangers of miscalculating the position of one's vessel, Admiral Sir Cloudesley Shovell, of the *Association*, ran his vessel aground on rocks off the Scilly Isles in 1707 during severe fog while believing

himself to be in safe waters. Three other ships of his fleet, the *Eagle,* the *Firebrand* and the *Romney*, were also wrecked, and all four vessels lost their entire complements, which numbered over 2,000 men.

Another perpetual hazard for ships' crews was that of fire. Certain regulations, such as restricting smoking to the upper decks, extinguishing all lights at night, and providing water buckets at strategic points were enforced to minimize the risk. If a fire did start, it was often impossible to put out, and if the guns had been kept loaded with powder they might begin to 'cook off', firing their shot randomly, or worse, at intended rescuers. Explosions could occur if the powder room was sparked, or if enemy attack set fire to it. Certain ships had an established drill to follow in the event of fire, whereby men would be assigned to certain areas, and water suction-pumped through hoses to attack the flames. In *The Fortune of War* Aubrey experiences the devastation of an explosion at first hand aboard HMS *La Flèche*, but he manages to survive and is rescued by HMS *Java.*

Leaking and shipping water were particular problems, especially in high seas. Ships were designed to draw together the water they had taken on into a pump well in the middle of the vessel, which was closely monitored to ensure that it remained within manageable limits. When necessary, pumps could be hand-operated to expel the water, but the work was hard and unpopular. However, if the winds were high and the vessel taking on water through pitching and rolling, very little could be done. Several vessels, including the *Java* mentioned above, as well as the *Blenheim*, disappeared without a trace while at sea, and with no survivors. Often, a captain's only recourse was to trim the sails as much as possible and ride out the gale, but if cannons became dislodged and rolled around below decks, or cargo and ballast shifted, then the masts might have been cut down to reduce topweight.

Abandoning ship was, predictably, a chaotic affair, and there seems to have been a common myth that in the event of a ship going down, the captain's authority no longer existed. This meant that many seamen ran riot, breaking into the liquor stores or raiding officers' rooms, ignoring orders and disabling any constructive efforts to save the ship. Aubrey witnesses such confusion in *Desolation Island*, when the *Leopard* hits an iceberg and, having raided the spirit-room, the men jump ship in a state of anarchy. The fact that many could not swim was perhaps lost on them in their inebriated state.

ROYAL NAVY VESSEL CASUALTIES IN 1799

Apollo	*Weazel*	*Prosperine*
Nautilus	*Grampus*	*Brave*
Les Deux Amis	*Contest*	*Trincomalee*
Blanche	*Fox*	*Lutine*
Impregnable	*Nassau*	*Orestes*
L'Espion	*Sceptre*	*Ethalion*
L'Amaranthe		

DATES AND DESCRIPTIONS OF HISTORICAL BATTLES AND OTHER SIGNIFICANT NAVAL EVENTS

3 January 1793 – The Anglo-French Wars commence when French batteries at Brest fire on HMS *Childers*. A month later France declares war on Britain and Holland.

21 May 1794 – Captain Horatio Nelson, alongside marines commanded by Lieutenant-Colonel Villettes, captures Bastia, Corsica, marking the beginning of Nelson's rise through the Royal Navy and of his naval renown.

1 June 1794 – The Glorious First of June was the first great fleet battle of the wars. Twenty-five ships-of-the-line, commanded by Admiral Earl Howe from his flagship HMS *Queen Charlotte*, defeat twenty-six French vessels led by Rear-Admiral Villaret-Joyeuse.

12 June 1794 – Nelson is blinded in his right eye while besieging Calvi, Corsica.

14 February 1797 – 1797 was a tumultuous year for the Royal Navy, with two great victories, but also two mutinies. The Battle of Cape St Vincent sees the British forces outnumbered by the Spanish, fifteen to twenty-seven; Nelson's presence at the battle, however, proves pivotal, for he engages seven enemy vessels, including the Spanish flagship, *Santissima Trinidad*, at that time the largest ship in the world. The Spanish are defeated with the loss of three thousand men compared to three hundred British seamen, and as a result of his actions Nelson is knighted. Aubrey is present at this battle in, variously, HMS *Orion*, as reported in *Post Captain*, and aboard HMS *Colossus* (*The Thirteen-Gun Salute*).

11 October 1797 – At the Battle of Camperdown, off the North Coast of Holland, Admiral Adam Duncan in HMS *Venerable* defeats the Dutch fleet, led by Vice-Admiral Jan de Winter in *Vrijheid*. While seeking to take advantage of the mutinous unrest in the Royal Navy earlier in the year, the Dutch were soundly beaten, with eleven of their vessels captured, as well as Admiral de Winter himself. In *Desolation Island* we learn that Aubrey was aboard the *Ardent* at the Battle of Camperdown.

1 August 1798 – The Battle of the Nile, (also known as Battle of Aboukir

Bay) is another crucial battle in the wars, isolating Napoleon's forces in Egypt – Nelson, commanding a fleet for the first time from HMS *Vanguard,* defeats Vice-Admiral François Brueys at Aboukir Bay. Demonstrating once again his aggressive tactics and extraordinary flair, Nelson not only attacks at night, catching the French off guard, but also manoeuvres his fleet between the French vessels and a nearby shoal – risking grounding in the shallower waters – and in doing so captures nine vessels caught at anchor and destroys two others.

18 February 1800 – Nelson's squadron captures one of the two French vessels to survive the Battle of the Nile, the 74-gun *Généreaux.* Prior to the opening of the first Aubrey-Maturin novel, *Master and Commander,* Jack Aubrey is involved in bringing *Généreaux* into port at Minorca (as the historical Captain Thomas Cochrane did) resulting (as it did for Cochrane) in Aubrey's promotion to commander.

2 April 1801 – The First Battle of Copenhagen takes place where the Danish fleet thought itself safest, at anchor in Denmark's chief port. After talks between the nations break down, Admiral Sir Hyde Parker, with Nelson second in command, orders the attack upon the anchored fleet; however, a number of key British vessels founder on the shoals

surrounding the harbour. What follows goes down in naval history; ignoring the heavy fire they are receiving, and the clear signalling of Admiral Parker to cease his bombardment, Nelson remarks, 'I have only one eye, I have a right to be blind sometimes. I really do not see that signal.' He continues the attack, the Danish fleet is defeated and surrenders, and the Royal Navy take twelve ships as prizes in return for handing over the Danish wounded.

6 May 1801 – The capture of the powerful Spanish frigate *El Gamo* by Captain Cochrane with his much smaller vessel, *Speedy,* is fictionalized in *Master and Commander* through the portrayal of Aubrey's capture of the *Cacafuego* with his small sloop-of-war, HMS *Sophie.* In turn, in the same novel on 3 July 1801, *Sophie* is taken by Admiral Linois, who in historical fact captured *Sophie*'s counterpart *Speedy.*

21 October 1805 – Eight leagues out from Cadiz, an outnumbered British force of twenty-seven ships-of-the-line led by the Admiral Lord Nelson blockades Admiral Villeneuve's combined Franco-Spanish fleet, comprising thirty-three vessels, in the most significant naval battle of the Napoleonic Wars. The Battle of Trafalgar is the culmination of a series of movements in which Napoleon hopes to clear the English Channel of any Royal Navy vessels in preparation for invading Britain. The navy's response to this is to blockade French ports, principally Toulon and Brest, the Textel and Rochefort. This allows them not only to restrict the

French fleet's movements, but gives the navy enough force to destroy the French should they put to sea. Nelson's tactic is to keep some distance from port, with only a small force visible from the French watchtowers, with the intention of luring the opposing vessels into combat. Meanwhile, it is observed that the Spanish are also amassing forces at their ports, particularly at El Ferrol, and this is confirmed when Spain declares war on Britain on 12 December 1804. Admiral Villeneuve breaks through the blockade at Toulon and heads across the Atlantic with Nelson in pursuit, but believing the latter's force to be greater than it is, doubles back on himself, meets up with the Spanish fleet from El Ferrol, and heads for Cadiz where he intends to refit and resupply. Aware that Nelson is waiting for him beyond the port, Villeneuve is hesitant to leave, and when ordered to do so by Napoleon on threat of a charge of cowardice, poor winds mean that few ships actually make it out of port and they have to return. However, this unintentional feint gives Nelson the upper hand, and he moves to close off the combined force's movement towards the Mediterranean, forcing them to give battle.

Despite the British fleet being outnumbered, through a combination of its superior morale, the highly trained and experienced crews manning its fleet, superior battle tactics, and Lord Nelson at the helm, the French and Spanish ships have no real expectation of victory. While waiting for the combined fleet to leave the port and make its way to combat, Nelson invites his fleet's captains over for dinner on the *Victory* to outline his new tactic. Known afterwards as 'The Nelson Touch', he plans to split, at right angles, the enemy force in two, concentrating one half of his firepower on the enemy rear, while blocking the remaining enemy ships coming to the aid of their comrades. It works brilliantly, and with battle commencing upon his famous declaration, 'England expects that every man will do his duty' (creating, it is reported, some consternation among the seamen with its implication that they might not have done their duty were it not for Nelson's provocation), the Battle of Trafalgar results in the destruction or capture of some twenty French and Spanish vessels, with no British ships lost. However, Nelson is shot and killed by a sniper as the *Victory* engages the *Redoutable*, but survives long enough to hear the news of his victory. The Royal Navy's victory at the Battle of Trafalgar all but destroys France's naval power, and secures British supremacy at sea for the next hundred years. Nelson was buried in St Paul's Cathedral, after a state funeral on 9 January 1806.

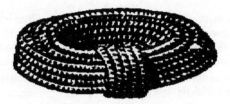

22 June 1807 – The US Navy originated during the War of Independence, and the Royal Navy's slow-burning conflict with the US was provoked partly by the disruption of American merchant vessels because of British blockades, and partly because of the navy's tendency to board American vessels to search for deserters – American citizens who had been impressed for service in the Royal Navy. Such a desertion occurs in June 1807, with a disagreement over the citizenship of four men. Having deserted from Royal Navy vessels anchored off the American coast, they are taken aboard the USS *Chesapeake*, at which the 50-gun fourth rate HMS *Leopard*, stationed nearby, demands their surrender. The *Chesapeake* naturally refuses, resulting in the *Leopard*'s captain, Salusbury Humphrey, giving the order to fire on the unsuspecting American vessel. Three US seamen are killed and eighteen injured, and the *Chesapeake* damaged, along with British and US diplomatic relations. Jack Aubrey is given command of the *Leopard* in O'Brian's *Desolation Island* and battles with the Dutch 74-gun *Waakzamheid*, on his way to restore order in New South Wales following the imprisonment of the ill-fated Captain William Bligh.

2 September 1807 – After demanding the surrender of the Danish fleet, the Second Battle of Copenhagen results in a joint naval and land-based bombardment under the command of Admiral Gambier. Copenhagen is severely damaged, and the Danish fleet destroyed.

August-December 1810 – A series of engagements around the island of Mauritius, colonized initially by the Dutch in the seventeenth century, but later proving to be a major thorn in the British side when occupied by the French, who harass the East India Company's merchant vessels. In August the French capture HMS *Neride* and HMS *Iphigenia*, and the Royal Navy burn HMS *Magicienne* and HMS *Iphigénie* to prevent their capture. In September, and under the command of Commodore Jacques Hamelin, the French ship *Venus* captures HMS *Ceylon*. In response, the

Royal Navy retaliates through the actions of Commodore Josias Rowley aboard HMS *Boadicea*, who destroys the *Venus*, killing Hamelin, and retakes the *Ceylon*. Mauritius falls to the British on 3 December; this action is fictionalized in *Mauritius Command*, where Jack Aubrey figures in Rowley's role in recovering the *Ceylon*, although O'Brian renames the captured vessel HMS *Bombay*.

1 June 1813 – After a series of US victories over the Royal Navy in preceding years, Captain James Lawrence of the 50-gun frigate USS *Chesapeake* perhaps allows his hubris to swell a little too large when he challenges HMS *Shannon*, a 38-gun frigate commanded by Captain Philip Broke, to single combat just outside Boston. However, the *Shannon* is known for its accomplished gunnery, and in the ensuing battle Lawrence is killed along with sixty of his crew, with eighty-five wounded. *Chesapeake* surrenders, and the victory is a rousing moral boost for the Royal Navy. Jack Aubrey finds himself at the heart of this battle aboard the *Shannon* in *The Fortune of War*.

16 October 1815 – After his defeat at Waterloo by Wellington, Napoleon is incarcerated on St Helena. HMS *Northumberland* carries him to the island where he will die almost six years later.

BLOCKADING

The act of blockading an enemy force was employed for several reasons. Firstly, it allowed Britain to keep watch over enemy fleets, to give an early warning should the fleet move or prepare to attack. Secondly, it denied an enemy fleet access to the open sea, removing its mobility and effectiveness. Thirdly, it applied a stranglehold to foreign trade, cutting off supplies and limiting enemy resources. The Royal Navy blockaded almost every port between the Baltic and Turkey, though the French ports and those of her allies occupied most of the navy's attention.

SOME FOREIGN NAVIES

French	Dutch	Spanish	American
Swedish	Russian	Turkish	

The Barbary States; namely, the forerunners to the modern countries of Morocco, Algeria, Tunisia and Libya.

COMBAT BETWEEN MEN-OF-WAR

Single-ship action

The victors of single-ship combat could not hope to expect to gain much in the way of prize money as this type of combat was devastating to both vessels involved. However, it was a notorious way of boosting the captain's honour and public esteem, and of inviting promotion.

Chasing

When threatened with defeat, retreat was always an option. Several factors needed to be considered in pursuit: in an open sea, the captain chasing would be at a disadvantage if his was a square-rigged ship chasing a fore-and-aft-rigged vessel; when chasing a vessel to windward, it was advisable to tack as soon as the chase was directly on the beam. Pursuing downwind, a captain would generally attempt to intersect the chase rather than follow directly, hoping not to lose his target through poor visibility or in darkness. If the captain in pursuit had a superior-handling vessel, his opponent would almost certainly want to hold a straight course, knowing that he could be out-tacked by the better ship. He could perhaps hope to lose his pursuer in poor visibility, or in darkness. A well-known retreat was staged by Admiral Cornwallis in 1795; vastly outnumbered, he misled his pursuers into believing that the rest of the British armada was just over the horizon by hoisting signals to the imaginary ships.

Raking
Raking the enemy meant to fire cannon at an enemy vessel's stern, which was the weakest part of the ship. The shot could easily penetrate the oak at that point and continue on through the ship, obliterating men and supplies, and potentially damaging and disrupting the target vessel's armament.

Range of combat
Though cannonades were sometimes used at long-range, once battle had been joined the combat was usually much closer, around 40 yards. However, the action between the *Mars* and the *Hercules* in 1794 was so close that the cannon muzzles could not be extended outside the ship, and the guns were fired from inside. A gap sufficient to allow the ship to be manoeuvred without colliding with the enemy was generally considered an ideal distance.

Broadside-to-broadside
The classic man-of-war combat position, vessels usually took up this attitude when one or other had failed to rake its opponent. The British tended to aim at the hull, while the French targeted the rigging – with the former having a far greater effect on the stability and condition of the vessel. Captain Broke, during the action with the *Chesapeake* (see p.101) is said to have exclaimed, 'Throw no shot away. Aim every one. Keep cool. Work steadily. Fire into her quarters. Don't try to dismast her. Kill the men, and the ship is yours.'

Boarding
Also a classic image in Georgian naval warfare, boarding was not usually employed in fleet actions, but more often used in single combat. It was also used when the opponent had been severely pounded already and its crew had probably sustained significant losses.

VICTORIES AND LOSSES

Between 1793 and 1815, the combined forces of Britain's enemies destroyed or captured 166 British warships, compared with 1,201 enemy vessels defeated by the Royal Navy. It is estimated that there were over 90,000 British naval deaths in the same period.

SURRENDER

To surrender a vessel was not a crime against Royal Naval Articles, but to do so without having offered sufficient or gallant opposition would often be punished severely. However, if the enemy force was overwhelming, then no more than a token gesture of defence might be offered, such as firing one salvo of cannon, before the surrendering vessel was boarded. To surrender, a vessel would haul down its ensign, and the victorious captain would often take his defeated rival's sword.

SHIPS AND THEIR CAPTAINS

Below are a few of the notable British commanders of Jack Aubrey's day:

Horatio Nelson (1758-1805)
HMS *Raisonnable* (Jack Aubrey served on the
Raisonnable in *The Mauritius Campaign*);
HMS *Lowestoffe*; HMS *Badger*;
HMS *Agamemnon* (his favourite vessel);
HMS *Captain*; HMS *Irresistible* (at the Battle of Cape
St Vincent); HMS *Victory* (at the Battle of Trafalgar)

Cuthbert Collingwood (1750-1810)
HMS *Royal Sovereign* (at the Battle of Trafalgar)

Richard Howe (1726-99)
HMS *Severn;* HMS *Triton*; HMS *Dunkirk,* HMS *Magnanime*; HMS *Queen Charlotte,* (at the Glorious First of June)

Thomas Cochrane (1775-1860)
HMS *Hind*; HMS *Barfleur*; HMS *Speedy* (Aubrey's HMS *Sophie* in *Master and Commander*)

RATES OF PAY OF A SHIP'S COMPLEMENT

Despite the fact that until 1797 common seamen had not had a pay rise since 1653, the rates of pay in the Royal Navy were still attractive in comparison with those of a land labourer. Even a landsman's pay would be tempting to young boys from poorer rural areas. As wages were paid irregularly and over long intervals (in wartime usually just before setting sail), seamen would often receive large amounts of cash – hence the prevalence of theft on board ship.

The first lieutenant of a ship decided the rating for each man and this, in turn, determined his duties and rate of pay. Wages were calculated on a lunar (28-day) month.

Actual rate of pay per annum in 1797:

Able seaman	£14 12s 6d	(24s per month)
Ordinary seaman	£11 7s 6d	(19s per month)
Landsman	£10 11s 6d	(17s 7d per month)

However, other wages had been rising steadily in the previous decades, including those of soldiers, many of whom served in the fleet. This disparity, together with general dissatisfaction with conditions of sea service, led to numerous petitions and the Spithead and Nore mutinies (see pp.90-1).

As a result, pay was increased by 5s 6d per lunar month for petty officers and able seamen, and by 4s 6d for lower rates. A further increase in 1806 meant that, before deductions, able seamen received 33s 6d per month, ordinary seamen 25s 6d, and landsmen 22s 6d.

Rank or Rating	Pay per Lunar Month	
	First Rate	**Sixth rate and under**[1,2]
Captain	£32 4s 6d	£16 6s 0d
Lieutenant[3]	£8 8s 0d	
Chaplain[4]	£11 10s 9d	
Surgeon[5]	£14 0s 0d	
Master[6]	£12 12s 0d	£7 7s 0d
Carpenter	£5 16s 0d	£3 1s 0d
Boatswain; gunner; purser	£4 16s 0d	£3 1s 0d
Master's mate	£3 16s 6d	£2 12s 6d
Midshipman	£2 15s 6d	£2 0s 6d
Captain's clerk	£4 7s 0d	£2 18s 6d
Schoolmaster; master-at-arms; armourer[7]	£2 15s 6d	£2 0s 6d
Carpenter's mate; caulker; ropemaker	£2 10s 6d	£2 0s 6d
Quartermaster; boatswain's/gunner's mates; yeoman of the powder room; corporal; armourer's mate	£2 5s 6d	£1 16s 6d
Sailmaker	£2 5s 6d	£2 0s 6d
Caulker's mate[8]	£2 6s 6d	
Yeoman of sheets; coxswain	£2 2s 6d	£1 16s 6d
Quartermaster's mate; captains of forecastle, foretop, main top, afterguard, and mast	£2 0s 6d	£1 15s 6d
Trumpeter	£2 0s 6d	£1 14s 6d
Quarter gunner; carpenter's crew	£1 16s 6d	£1 15s 6d
Gunsmith; steward[9]	£1 15s 6d	£1 9s 6d
Cook	£1 15s 6d	£1 14s 6d
Able seaman	£1 13s 6d	
Ordinary seaman	£1 5s 6d	
Landsman	£1 2s 6d	

(Source: O'Neill, Patrick O'Brian's Navy)

[1]In many cases the rate of pay varied in a decreasing scale according to the rating of the ship from first-rate (maximum) to sixth-rate and below (minimum). The second and third columns therefore represent the maximum and minimum for each rank. Where there is a figure in the second column and none in the third, this indicates that the rate of pay was standard, regardless of the ship's rating.

[2]Amounts are expressed in nineteenth-century English money, where the figures represent pounds (£), shillings (s), and pence (d); i.e., £3 14s 6d = three pounds, fourteen shillings, and sixpence. The system was that 12 pence = 1 shilling (s); 20 shillings = 1 pound (£).

[3]Pay of lieutenant in a flagship was enhanced by 14s 0d per month.

[4]Chaplains on first to fifth rates only. Could also act as schoolmaster, in which case he earned the appropriate bonus and capitation rate (see Note 7)

[5]Surgeon's rates depended upon length of service: 6 years: £14 0s 0d; 7-9 years: £15 8s 0d; 10-19 years: £19 12s 6d; 20 years: £25 4s 0d.

[6]£6 6s 6d for second masters in brigs, sloops and cutters.

[7]Schoolmasters also earned an annual bonus of £20 plus capitation rate of £5 per pupil.

[8]Caulker's mate in first to fourth rates only.

[9]Gunsmith in first to third rates only.

DEDUCTIONS FROM PAY

All seamen	6d per month to the Greenwich Hospital
All seamen	2d for the surgeon
Warrant officers	1s per month to the Chatham Chest, a fund for distressed seamen
Officers	3d per pound per annum for the Officers' Widows Fund
Seamen earning over £60 p.a.	From 1799, income tax on a sliding scale; highest rate 2s in the £ for salaries over £150
Clothing and other items	Various

METHODS OF PAYMENT

Wages were often paid in arrears to deter desertion. When the ship was finally paid off the seamen could expect to get their pay. On a foreign voyage, as in wartime, the crew was normally paid before setting out as encouragement to the men to make the journey.

Ships could be in commission on foreign service for years, so seamen would often receive a substantial amount in back pay on their return. They could opt to have part of their wages deducted at source to be paid directly to their dependants. If men were transferred (turned over) to another ship, or sent to hospital before their ship was paid, they were issued with tickets. There was often a prolonged delay before these were cashed by the navy and some men traded them privately at a discounted rate to get their hands on some money.

The day of payment in a home dockyard was always a scene of bustling activity. As each man's name was called out, he would go forward and offer his hat, which was then returned to him with his wages inside and the amount chalked on the rim. Women and traders gathered at the port to offer their wares to the newly flush seamen.

PRIZE MONEY

Navy recruitment posters often used the lure of riches in the form of prize money. In reality, however, most common seamen saw little of the spoils of plundering as the majority was distributed between the officers, at least until 1808. After that date the entire crew was allowed a quarter share of the whole haul.

Division of prize money after 1808

Midshipmen/senior petty officers	$4^1/2$ shares each
Junior petty officers	3 shares each
Able/ordinary seamen	$1^1/2$ shares each
Landsmen/servants	1 share each
Boys	$^1/2$ share each

HALF-PAY

Common seamen belonged to a particular ship, not the navy. When not attached to a ship they received no pay. Officers, on the other hand, were entitled to half-pay while awaiting a new ship or commission. They often actually received more than half their normal pay. For example, the lowest half-pay rate was 5s a day, whereas a lieutenant earned 6s a day while at sea. Some lieutenants even received the full half-pay rate of 7s a day – more than they earned when working!

The rates of half-pay were calculated according to seniority rather than on the rating of the officer's last ship. In 1815 half-pay was paid quarterly.

APPENDIX:

PATRICK O'BRIAN AND
THE AUBREY-MATURIN NOVELS

Patrick O'Brien (1914-2000)

Born Richard Patrick Russ in Buckinghamshire, UK (and not Ireland, as was commonly thought), Patrick O'Brian seemed destined to become a novelist when he published his first work, *Caesar*, at the age of fifteen. Before writing the 'Aubrey-Maturin' series, however, he was to pen more 'mainstream' fiction, including *Testimonies* (1950) and *The Catalans* (1953), as well as translations of such French writers as Simone de Beauvoir and André Maurois (*Papillon*). He first turned his hand to naval fiction in 1956 with *The Gold Ocean* and followed with *The Unknown Shore* (1959), but it was to be ten years before O'Brian released the first novel of one of the most extraordinary sagas in modern fiction.

Master and Commander introduced Jack Aubrey and his companion Stephen Maturin to a reading public already familiar with nautical authors such as Alexander Kent, C.S. Forester and Frederick Marryat. However, despite critical acclaim, mass popularity eluded O'Brian until 1989, when an American publisher picked up *The Reverse of the Medal* (1986) and the series became a publishing phenomenon. Lauded as a stylistic cross between Anthony Trollope and Jane Austen, refiguring Austen's class concerns through the complications and tensions of naval hierarchy, with a driving force of historical narrative and a fine perception of character, detail and dialogue, O'Brian's fiction finally achieved the critical – and public – acclaim which it deserved. Having lived in France for much of this life, O'Brian died in January 2000 while living in Dublin. He left unfinished a half-completed manuscript of the twenty-first Aubrey-Maturin novel, which has yet to be published.

The Aubrey-Maturin novels

Master and Commander	(1969)
Post Captain	(1972)
HMS Surprise	(1973)
The Mauritius Command	(1977)
Desolation Island	(1978)
The Fortune of War	(1979)
The Surgeon's Mate	(1980)
The Ionian Mission	(1981)
Treason's Harbour	(1983)
The Far Side of the World	(1984)
The Reverse of the Medal	(1986)
The Letter of Marque	(1988)
The Thirteen-Gun Salute	(1989)
The Nutmeg of Consolation	(1991)
Clarissa Oakes (US: *The Truelove*)	(1992)
The Wine-Dark Sea	(1993)
The Commodore	(1995)
The Yellow Admiral	(1997)
The Hundred Days	(1998)
Blue at the Mizzen	(1999)

GLOSSARY: SOME TERMS USED IN THE ROYAL NAVY IN JACK AUBREY'S TIME

Able seaman: a knowledgeable sailor.

Afore: to the front of the vessel.

Aft: to the rear of the vessel.

Afterguard: a body of men at work on the quarterdeck and poop.

Aloft: above decks; up in the masts or rigging.

Amidships: in the centre part of the vessel.

Astern: behind.

Athwart: across.

Ballast: a type of weight carried in the bottom of a ship's hold to keep the vessel stable; usually made of pig iron, stones or gravel.

Bar: shallow water in the entrance to harbour.

Barque: a three-masted ship.

Batten down: to close and secure the ship's hull and deck openings to prevent the entry of water and air.

Beam: width of ship.

Bear a hand: offer help.

Bear away: to change direction to sail before the wind.

Bilge: the angle of the ship's hull between bottom and side.

Bilges: the bottom compartment of a ship, usually filled with waste water.

Binnacle: a locker, positioned in front of the ship's wheel, containing the steering compass.

Block: a pulley.

Boarding nets: nets strung out from a ship's side to stop boarding.

Boatswain: a ship's officer in charge of equipment and the crew.

Bomb vessel (or bomb): a small warship designed to carry one or two heavy mortars for attacks on the shore.

Bounty: amount of money paid as a reward or financial inducement for completion of a task.

Bowlines: ropes attached to sails to pull them forward.

Bowsprit: a spar at the front of a ship that projects over the bow; also known as a boltsprit.

Box haul: sharp turning of a ship.

Brace: a rope used to hold direction of a sail.

Brigantine: a two-masted, square-rigged ship; also known as a brig.

Bring to: to direct a ship into the wind so that it slows down and almost stops; also known as 'heave to'.

Broadside: the entire battery positioned on one side of a ship; also, the simultaneous fire of every broadside gun.

Bulkhead: an internal vertical partition in a vessel.

Burgoo: a type of porridge.

Buss: a two-masted fishing vessel.

Cable: heavy rope.

Cable (length): 240 yards.

Cable tier: section of the orlop deck where the anchor cables were kept.

Capstan: a large cylindrical device into which sailors inserted sturdy poles for rotating, which enabled them to haul up unwieldy cables.

Careen: to lie a ship on its side to allow its hull to be cleaned or repaired; also known as 'heaving down'.

Cat: to lift an anchor from the water to the level of the forecastle.

Caulking: a system of using unpicked rope and pitch to seal gaps in planks.

Clean: to bream (remove shells or weeds from) and scrape the bottom of a ship, either by careening or while in dock.

Close-hauled: rigging a ship to sail directly into the wind.

Cutter: a single-masted small ship rigged with a gaff mainsail, headsails and usually a square topsail.

Driver: the main mast of a brig; also a gaff sail set on the mizzen mast of a vessel.

En flute: a warship without some, or all, of its cannon.

Fish: to mend a broken or damaged spar by attaching another spar to its side to act as a splint.

Flag officer: an admiral.

Fleet: a group of merchant ships.

Fore: the front of a ship.

Forecastle: the small deck at the front of ship.

Frigate: a fifth- or sixth-rate warship; a ship-rigged sloop carrying 16–18 guns; also describes any small cruising warship.

Gaff: a yard supporting the top of certain sails.

Gasket: a plaited rope holding sails to yards.

Ground tackle: cable, anchors, and the equipment used to lift them.

Halyards: ropes to raise or lower sails, yards or flags.

Hand: to gather in the squaresails.

Haul off: to move away from land or from another ship.

Heads: the crew's latrines.

Jib: a triangular sail at the bow of a ship.

Keel: a type of square-rigged sailing barge.

Landfall: the place at which a vessel at sea meets the coast.

Landsman: an inexperienced sailor.

Larboard: port.

Lateen sail: a triangular sail.

Lee shore: a shore towards which the wind blows a vessel.

Leeward: in the direction towards which the wind is blowing.

Let go: to free or cast off; also to drop anchor.

Log-line: a long rope, knotted at various intervals, attached to a piece of wood that is thrown into the sea, which measures a ship's speed based on the number of knots that pass in a measured period of time.

Luff: to turn a ship closer to the wind.

Lug sail: a four-sided sail.

Lying to: the position a ship is in after being brought to.

Mast: a vertical spar that supports sails, yards, gaffs and spars. Ships had three masts, comprising fore (towards the front of the ship), main (the tallest) and mizzen (the aftermost mast); a brigantine had just fore and main masts; a ketch had main and mizzen masts.

Midshipmen: junior-ranking officers responsible for helping with the control of the crew and other duties.

Muster: a list of names of people on board a ship.

Offing: the view of the open sea from land.

Ordinary seaman: a sailor with limited experience.

Orlop deck: the lowest deck on a vessel, on the same level as or below the waterline.

Packet: a small, fast ship used for sending despatches and orders.

Pay off: to decommission a ship and discharge her crew.

Petty officer: a term describing various seamen including gunner's mates, quartermasters, masters-at-arms, sailmakers, surgeon's mates, carpenters, boatswain's mates and coopers.

Pinnace: a ship's boat.

Pipe: to give an order, especially when a call is issued from a boatswain's whistle.

Pitch: the movement of a ship when the stern and head plunge alternately into the sea.

Plying: turning to windward.

Point: to position the head of a vessel in a specific direction, relative to the wind.

Poop: a short deck built above the after (rear) end of the quarterdeck.

Pull: to row.

Quarterdeck: a deck above the main deck that runs from the stern to midway along the length of the vessel.

Rate: one of six classifications of man-of-war vessels – first rates had the greatest number of guns, sixth rates had the least.

Rating: a member of a ship's company without a naval rank.

Ratlines: a series of small lines of rope fastened across a ship's shrouds and used as a ladder to climb the rigging.

Reef: to reduce the area of a sail by gathering and tying sections of it.

Rigging: the action of providing a vessel with sails, braces and stays.

Royal: a squaresail positioned beneath the topgallant mast.

Run: to leave a ship without permission; to desert.

Sheets: ropes attached to bottom corners of sails, and used to control them.

Ship: a square-rigged vessel with three masts.

Shrouds: support ropes running from the masts to the ship's sides.

Sloop: a small man-of-war of a classification lower than sixth-rate.

Spar: a thick strong pole or length of timber from which sails are hung.

Square-rigged: a ship rigged with horizontal squaresails at its masts.

Stays: fore-and-aft support ropes required for the masts.

Stockfish: dried cod.

Stream: a current; also the part of a harbour in which currents flow.

Strike: to run aground.

Tack: directing a ship into and through the wind or turning it by steering to windward; also, a ship's course relative to the direction of the wind.

Top: the platform around the lower mast, providing a place for men to work aloft.

Topgallant: the highest of the three spars used to make a mast.

Topman: a sailor who works aloft.

Turn: to tack.

Wardroom: an area set aside for use as the commissioned officers' mess.

Watch: a fixed period of duty lasting a few hours.

Way: a ship's movement through the water.

Wear: to turn a ship by moving the bow in the direction of the wind.

Weather: to sail to windward of a cape or other feature.

Windage: the extent to which a ship is blown off course by the wind.

Windward: in the direction from which the wind is blowing.

Yard: a horizontal spar suspended from a mast that holds up the sails.

Yardarm: outer section of the yard.

BIBLIOGRAPHY AND SOURCES

Books

NICHOLAS BLAKE and RICHARD LAWRENCE, *The Illustrated Companion to Nelson's Navy: A Guide to the Fiction of the Napoleonic Wars*, London, Chatham Publishing, 2000

DEAN KING, *Harbours and High Seas: An Atlas and Geographical Guide to the Complete Aubrey-Maturin Novels of Patrick O'Brian*, New York, Owl Books, 2003

DEAN KING *et al.*, *A Sea of Words: A Lexicon and Companion to the Complete Seafaring Tales of Patrick O'Brian*, New York, Owl Books, 2000

BRIAN LAVERY, *Nelson's Navy: The Ships, Men and Organisation, 1793-1815*, London, Conway Maritime Press, 1995

PATRICK O'BRIAN, *Men of War: Life in Nelson's Navy*, New York, W. W. Norton, 1995

RICHARD O'NEILL, (ed.) *Patrick O'Brian's Navy: The Illustrated Companion to Jack Aubrey's World*, Philadelphia, Running Press, 2003

N. A. M. RODGER, *The Wooden World: An Anatomy of the Georgian Navy*, London, Fontana, 1988

JOHN TERRAINE, *Trafalgar*, London, Sidgwick & Jackson, 1976

All of these are not only first-rate books (to use a nautical expression) but also excellent sources of information (with, in some cases, magnificent illustrations) about the Georgian Royal Navy in the period covered by Patrick O'Brian's Aubrey-Maturin novels. Those novels are listed in the Appendix (pp.111-12); they are published by HarperCollins in the UK, and by W. W. Norton in the USA.

Websites

Besides literally hundreds of books about the Royal Navy of the time, and ancillary subjects, there are a great many websites that deal, in part or in whole, with the subject. It is not possible to list all the many excellent websites, on which can be found anything from the muzzle-velocity and penetration of a 32-pounder long gun to details of amputations carried out at sea, but below are some of the best.

> www.nelsonsnavy.co.uk
> www.hmssurprise.org
> www.cronab.demon.co.uk
> www.hms.org.uk
> www.aboutnelson.co.uk
> www.history.navy.mil
> www.hms-trincomalee.co.uk
> www.nmm.ac.uk
> www.hms-victory.com
> www.ussconstitution.navy.mil
> www.napoleonguide.com/navy

Museums and ships

Finally, mention must be made of the wonderful collections in the National Maritime Museum at Greenwich, London, and the Royal Naval Museum at Portsmouth, as well as of three surviving men-of-war from those days, all of which can be visited. The first of these, HMS *Victory*, the 100-gun first rate that was Nelson's flagship at Trafalgar, is in dry dock at Portsmouth; launched in 1765, she is the oldest warship in the world still in commission, and serves as the flagship of the Second Sea Lord and C-in-C Naval Home Command. The second, equally famous, warship is the 44-gun American frigate USS *Constitution* – 'Old Ironsides' – at Boston, Massachusetts, which still serves with the US Navy and is the oldest commissioned warship still afloat. Finally, HMS *Trincomalee*, a 38-gun frigate of the *Leda* class, although not quite contemporary with the period (having been launched in 1817), is very similar to some of the warships on which Jack Aubrey served; now at Hartlepool, she has been superbly restored, and is the second oldest warship still afloat. There are good official websites for all three vessels, and these are given above.

INDEX